A SEASON OF
Birthing
Unlocking The Power Within

Kenisha B. Moore

A Season of Birthing
Unlocking The Power Withing
Copyright © 2021 Kenisha B. Moore

TRU Statement Publications supports the right to free expression and the value of copyright. The purpose of copyright is to encourage writers and artist to produce the creative works that will leave a timeless impression of humanity.

The scanning, uploading, reproduction, and distribution of this book, in any form, stored in a retrieval system, or transmitted in any form by any means—electric, mechanical, photocopy, recording, or otherwise—without prior written permission of the author, except as provided by United States of America copyright law, is a theft of the author's intellectual property. If you would like permission to use materials from the book (other than for a review), please contact kbmoore23@gmail.com

Thank you for your support of the author's rights. For more information about the author and other works, visit www.kenishabmoore.com

Amplified Bible (AMP) Copyright © 2015 by The Lockman Foundation, La Habra, CA 90631. All rights reserved. THE HOLY BIBLE, NEW INTERNATIONAL VERSION®, NIV® Copyright © 1973, 1978, 1984, 2011 by Biblica, Inc.® Used by permission. All rights reserved worldwide. Scripture taken from the New King James Version®. Copyright © 1982 by Thomas Nelson. Used by permission. All rights reserved. Scripture quotations marked NLT are taken from the Holy Bible, New Living Translation, copyright © 1996, 2004, 2015 by Tyndale House Foundation. Used by permission of Tyndale House Publishers, Inc., Carol Stream, Illinois 60188. All rights reserved. Scripture taken from The Voice™. Copyright © 2008 by Ecclesia Bible Society. Used by permission. All rights reserved. Scripture quotations marked MSG are taken from THE MESSAGE, copyright © 1993, 2002, 2018 by Eugene H. Peterson. Used by permission of NavPress. All rights reserved. Represented by Tyndale House Publishers, Inc.

Other Reference Sources: Bible Gateway, dictionary.com, Merriam-webster.com, Oxford Languages, yourdictionary.com, Mark Tittley's A Manual for Worship Leaders, Wikipedia, the free encyclopedia: Glorification (theology)

Cover design by Triv Enterprise, LLC www.bytriv.com | contact@bytriv.com

Book Completion Services Provided by:
TRU Statement Publications | www.trustatementpublications.com

First Edition: May 2021
Printed in the United States of America
0 5 2 2 2 0 2 1
ISBN: 978-1-948085-56-4

MESSAGE FROM *the Author*

I take absolutely no credit for anything that has taken place in my life. All Glory and Honor belongs to GOD the FATHER for "THE PLAN" JESUS CHRIST the Son of God for "SALVATION to Fulfill the Plan" And HOLY SPIRIT for "Carrying Out the Plan." GOD has a plan for your life too!

It begins with receiving His plan of REDEMPTION, through SALVATION, by FAITH in JESUS CHRIST. You are about to read a portion of the plan he had for my life. As you read the pages of this book, you Will be Empowered to pursue His plan for your life!

Disclaimer: This is not a Self-Help Book. It is a Divine Discovery that will result in Impartation and Activation.

> *Revelation 3:8 (MSG): I see what you've done. Now see what I've done. I've opened a door before you that no one can slam shut. You don't have much strength, I know that; you used what you had to keep my Word. You didn't deny me when times were rough.*

Dedication

This book is dedicated to my beloved husband, William Moore, whom I love dearly! Thank you for enduring the process to the best of your ability and for obeying God by making it right!
I appreciate you and I thank God for our union!

Thank you to all others who contributed in some way to this process and the completion of this book. You know who you are!

God Bless!

TABLE OF *Contents*

Prologue i
Introduction iii
PART 1 ....
  A SEASON OF BIRTHING ....
    Who Summoned Me? 1
    Hidden Mystery 7
    Labor? Not in vain! 11
    "Shhh!" Test in Progress 15
    No Smooth Sailing 21
    Catch the Wind 27
  UNVEILING DESTINY ....
    Don't You Drown That Baby 33
    Summary of 2008-2010 43
    Peace! Be Still! 47
    Prophetic 2012 & 2013 53
    School of Warfare 59
    The Calm Before The Storm 67
    Temporary Turbulence 71
    The Inevitable Storm 79
    You Don't Need A Doctor, Remember? 87

You Don't Have to Force What God Has Ordained..........................
Summary of 2015-2019.. 97
PERFECT VISION: *20/20*... 103
PART 2: THE POWER KEYS ....
Unlocking The Power Within – The Power Keys 109
Power Key #1: The "Yes" 111
Power Key #2: Obedience 115
Power Key #3: Faith... 119
Power Key #4: Observation 125
Power Key #5: The "Wait" 129
Power Key #6: Worship 133
Power Key #7: Glorification 139
Power Key #8: The Master Key 145

Prologue

I began writing this book on October 22, 2013, after receiving instructions from The Lord a few weeks prior. I knew several years ago that I had to write a book about my experience. The original title of this book was "Birthing Amiracle: Memoirs of Kenisha," but after 7 years, I was inspired to give it a new title.

I actually thought the book would be written after the process of this plan was complete. Well, I was definitely wrong. As I am writing right now, we are still waiting on the complete manifestation of the promise. How am I writing a book about something that hasn't happened yet? It's called FAITH!

Hebrews 11:1 (AMP): Now faith is the assurance (the confirmation, the title deed) of the things [we] hope for, being the proof of things [we] do not see and the conviction of their reality [faith perceiving as real fact what is not revealed to the senses].

A SEASON OF BIRTHING *Unlocking the Power Within*

Introduction

My name is Kenisha Moore, I am the wife of William Moore, whom I refer to as Tony throughout this book. As you turn the pages, you are about to embark on a journey through a series of events that have taken place for about 15 years. The first half of this book is written from a journal that I kept over a span of time, while the second half gives you Eight Powerful Keys to assist you in Unlocking Your Power. I ask that you keep an open mind and heart as I allow you into an intimate space to revisit this journey with me. I also ask that you read the book in its entirety, to get a full understanding of the experience.

I was 24 years old, pregnant with our second child, and working at a Technical College teaching Cosmetology. There was a young lady named Teresa, a student of mine whom I'd met on several occasions before she actually became my student. The first time we met was on campus at Georgia Southern University through a mutual friend. About two years later, she signed up to take Cosmetology, and I would've been her teacher if the class had not been canceled for the lack of students. Less than a year later in 2002, we met again in a totally different city, at a completely different college, and I still ended up being her teacher. Now that's what I call a divine connection!

There was one particular night while the students were working on their manikins, Teresa came and told me that she had a dream about me. It went something like this, "Mrs. Moore, I had a dream about you: I had gotten married and moved away. You and I lost contact and didn't communicate for a while, but I'm not sure why. You ran into my grandmother somewhere and we reconnected. We followed you to your house, which was a long way out. I remember seeing a lot of trees and an address with zeros in it. There was also something green that caught my attention. One part of the house was set up like a salon where you could do hair. I went inside of the house and there were two boys, Kameron, and I didn't know who the little one was. The little one said to me, 'Do you want to come see my sister?' I went down a long hallway and followed him into a room. There in the room was a tiny baby girl, lying in a crib."

Now, keep in mind that I was pregnant with our second child at the time. I looked at her with excitement that the child I was carrying could possibly be a girl. Well, after my doctor's visit, I found out that I was having another boy. About five months later, Keelan Moore was born. Our oldest son, Kameron Moore, was two years old at the time. We accepted the fact that we had two boys whom we love dearly and were perfectly fine with not having a daughter.

PART 1
The Journal

A SEASON OF BIRTHING
Who Summoned Me?

June 23, 2005

Dr. Juanita Bynum was hosting a summit called, "Women on the Front Line." Today is my 27th birthday, and I was so excited that I called Teresa to tell her about my plans to go. She told me that God was going to do several things for me while attending the summit. On June 29, 2005, my mother, my aunt, and a lady from our church drove to Tampa, Florida. Dr. Cindy Trimm was also a speaker at the summit. The definition of Summit is the highest level, importance, or rank: a meeting of chiefs of governments or other high officials. This was clearly not a regular conference. It was a summoning of a select group of people to attend, and I knew I had to be there.

June 30, 2005

The second night of the summit: After the message was delivered, Dr. Trimm gave us very specific instructions before she released a prophetic declaration. She told us to get really close together, shoulder to shoulder with the people next to us. She began to explain that God was about to release a "Kingdom Millionaire" anointing that was only going to hit a select group of people. She told us we would feel something like an earthquake, but not to get emotional. She also told us that this special anointing was going to skip over some people and only hit the select group.

As Dr. Trimm began to pray, my body began to tremble. The more it trembled, the more I tried to stop it, but I couldn't. I remember thinking to myself, "Uh oh, what's happening to me! No emotions, no emotions!" While she was making decrees and declarations, all of a sudden, I felt something hit me like a large tidal wave. The next thing I knew, I was sliding down the metal chair in slow motion like a low tide coming onto the seashore. I stopped midway, frozen into a position with my back up against the seat of the chair, my behind not quite touching the floor, and my legs extended out in front of me. In that moment, I felt paralyzed as I was in that position for every bit of three minutes! I'd never experienced anything like it before! While I was on the floor, I remember receiving a new prayer language, which was very exciting to me, because I was always in a place of wanting more from God.

July 1, 2005

Today was the third day of the summit. As I was participating in praise and worship, singing and clapping, all of a sudden, I realized my hands became really cold. So, I started rubbing them together, trying to create friction to warm them up. This went on for about five minutes, but it wasn't helping at all because my hands were still extremely cold. I continued rubbing them together as I was singing. A few minutes later, I noticed my ears had become really hot. So, I put my extremely cold hands over my flaming hot ears, but nothing seemed to cool them. Not concerned about what was happening, I continued to praise and worship God.

About fifteen minutes later, after my hands and ears returned to normal, I felt a thump in my stomach. This thump continued at random times and I said to myself, "I must have gas." After several minutes, I went to the restroom to try to release what I thought was gas, as I continued to feel this random thump.

Upon coming back into the conference area once the speaker was done, we began to pray corporately. As I was on my knees, I heard God clearly speak to my spirit and say, *"When your hands were cold, I gave you the power of healing. When your ears were hot, I opened them up for you to hear Me clearly."*

I was ecstatic, I had been praying and desiring for so long to hear the Voice of God and I experienced it on my last night of the summit!

When we got back to the hotel, I went to take a shower. While in the shower, I heard God speak to me again! He said to me, *"You are pregnant."*

I immediately thought back to the thumping that I felt earlier at the summit and was still feeling at random intervals throughout the night. When I got out of the shower, I didn't say a word to anyone. I barely slept that night, trying to process everything that happened those three nights. I couldn't wait to get back home so I could tell Tony!

July 2, 2005

Saturday: We arrived back in Georgia. Once I made it home, I told Tony all about the events that took place and the things I heard God say to me. My husband is not a man of many words, so he just nodded as he listened. I even called Teresa and told her about everything. She told me she already knew I would receive the gift of healing and that she really wasn't surprised. Within a few hours of arriving home, I went and purchased a pregnancy test. I went to the bathroom at home, took the test, and waited for the results. Well, to my surprise, the outcome was negative. Of course, now I'm a little puzzled.

July 3, 2005

The next day, my cousins Vonaye and Shawn came home with me after church. Before we went to my house, we rode around looking at new houses and neighborhoods all day. This was something we liked to do on a regular basis. We would go to the gated communities for the open houses to ride through and look at the beautiful homes. As we were riding, I began to tell them about my experience at the summit. Even though they were both teenagers, we would always have conversations about the bible and spiritual matters.

That night, once we got home and settled down, Vonaye, the eldest sister, began having a vision. She saw a beautiful house and described it in very vivid details, even down to the cars in the garage. She also saw me traveling and doing hair for someone who is famous, as I was not working at the college anymore. Vonaye also said she saw a little girl in a diaper running through the house. She then interpreted what happened at the summit, as a spiritual *Tsunami*: An earthquake in the ocean floor that causes massive waves.

Now, keep in mind, I said nothing to them about Dr. Trimm mentioning an earthquake. But she took it a step further and interpreted it as a Tsunami and the way I slid down over the chair was like a wave. Let me remind you that this is a teenager having a vision for the first time. Vonaye was excited, yet also startled at what she was seeing. This was definitely only by the Spirit of God!

July 4, 2005

The next morning, Shawn, the younger sister, noticed a picture we've had for years hanging on the wall. It says, "God Bless Our Home." She brought our attention to the church and the house in the picture.

The significance of this relates to a dream by the husband of an old friend of mine. I never met her husband, but he had a dream about me and my husband. In the latter part of 2004, she called me and told me the dream: "You and your husband were coming to visit us and in my husband's dream. Your name came up on the Caller ID. He spelled your name out because he didn't know who you were. You all came into our house and my husband heard a voice say, 'In your houses, will be pillars.'"

The dream was confirmed when I was riding to work, listening to my Bible CD's one day and a portion of this scripture caught my attention: 1 Timothy 3:15 (NIV), "In the HOUSE of God, which is the church of the living God, the PILLAR and foundation of the truth." The dream was both natural and spiritual, thus the picture Shawn pointed out with the Church (spiritual house) and the House (natural house).

A SEASON OF BIRTHING *Unlocking the Power Within*

Hidden Mystery

July 5, 2005

Three days after returning home, I went to my doctor. I was administered a urine test and a blood test to check for pregnancy hormones. The next morning, I received a phone call about the results of the tests, and guess what they were—Yes, NEGATIVE!

July 14, 2005

A little over a week later, I had an ultrasound performed. Now keep in mind, I still feel the random thumps that are now more like tiny kicks. Before the ultrasound, I had to sign a form stating, if the ultrasound doesn't find anything, I am responsible for the bill. So, guess what the ultrasound revealed—NOTHING! Sure enough, I had to write a check because our insurance wouldn't cover it.

I swiftly walked out of the doctor's office, got in the elevator calmly and composed, but as soon as I got in my car and sat down behind the steering wheel, I immediately burst into tears! While sitting there, I cried for a few minutes because I couldn't understand why this was happening. As I got myself together and turned the ignition switch to start the car, my Bible CD began to play as it normally did. However, this time as soon as it came over the car speaker, I heard:

"Leave her alone! She is in bitter distress, but the Lord has hidden it from me and has not told me why." "Did I ask you for a son, my lord? she said. Didn't I tell you, don't raise my hopes?" 2 Kings 4:27-28 (NIV).

One version says, "Did I not say, do not deceive me?" Astonished at what I was hearing, I turned the volume up and replayed it at least five more times. It was the story of the Shunamite woman, who prepared a place to stay for the prophet Elisha whenever he came to the area. In return for her hospitality, Elisha prophesied that she would have a child. She was troubled in this particular passage because her son died. Feeling deceived, she reminded him that she didn't ask for a child. This is EXACTLY how I felt at that moment in my car! I didn't ask to have another child. God had spoken to me, and I was just standing in faith for what He spoke.

While still sitting in the car, I heard God say, *"And you don't need a doctor."* Of course, at this point, I'm really perplexed.

The passage of scripture playing, as soon as I started my car, was not a coincidence. This was God's divine timing! If you read the entire story of the Shunamite woman in 2 Kings 4:8-37, you will find that the son was miraculously raised back to life.

I went to the doctor on my lunch break from work. When I got back to work I told a co-worker what happened and I asked her to pray with me. As she was praying, she saw a vision. She said to me, "I see you standing at a podium, on a round stage, speaking to an audience with hundreds of people. As you are speaking, you go behind the curtain and bring out a little girl. The crowd begins to roar, applauding as she holds your hand and walks to the front of the stage. She looks about three years old. She has on a black velvet dress with a white sailor like collar, white lace socks and black shoes. Her hair has ponytails with little twists in the ponytails. She looks kind of like this one (pointing at the three-year-old Kameron in a picture of Keelan and him on my desk), but with ponytails and a little darker in complexion." This moment sparked my faith a little bit more!

July 15, 2005

The next day was a beautiful day. Driving home from work was absolutely serene and peaceful. We lived out in the country, so the drive was long and full of nature scenes and countryside. As I was driving down the highway, I suddenly looked up to the sky, and to my surprise saw a cloud shaped like a baby, with a bottle in its mouth. This shape, which was like a silhouette side view, only lasted about 15 seconds and then slowly disappeared. It was one of the most amazing things I'd ever seen! I wish I could have taken a picture of it, but it happened so quickly. I was in awe because The Almighty God shaped a cloud just for me. Wow!

July 24, 2005

A select group of people believed me. Tony somewhat believes, but he's just not completely sure. A few others think I'm pregnant with or birthing something spiritual. That makes sense also, but why would several people have visions and dreams about a little girl, so I'm going to continue to believe God and walk by faith daily.

Around the middle of August 2005, God started dealing with us about moving. We lived in Waynesboro, my hometown, which is a small town outside of Augusta, Georgia. I felt like God was dealing with us the way He dealt with Abraham, when He told him in Genesis 12:1 (NKJV): "Get out of your country, from your family and from your father's house to a land that I will show you." We had no idea where we were going to move to, but we knew to get prepared. So, in faith, we started packing. Just about every weekend, Vonaye, Shawn, the boys and I would ride around looking for a house.

August 26, 2005

I was styling my aunt's hair and told her that we were looking for a house in Augusta. She then tells me she and her husband have a house they are getting prepared to rent out. She mentioned the address, which had two zeros in it. She also told me about an odd green colored carpet. There was even a building, wired with electricity, in the backyard. My mind immediately went to Teresa's dream.

Now, keep in mind that I still feel the random kicks. But I took a third pregnancy test on August 28, 2005, which was our Wedding Anniversary. I also have regular menstrual cycles.

Labor? Not in vain!

September 18, 2005

We are moving in two weeks. I have no idea what we're going to do with the house we have now: Walking by Faith!

September 26, 2005

I told my mother-in-law about the baby, and she told me that she saw a baby in the clouds the day before. Moving has been pushed back a few weeks. I estimate the middle of October around the 15th. I'm excited about Ke'Lani. I estimate my due date to be November 7 – 8.

As a result of Teresa's dream, my co-worker, and Vonaye's visions, I knew I was having a girl. As I researched and looked up baby names and meanings, I came across the name "Okeilani," which means "from Heaven." It is Hawaiian in origin. Since both our boys' name begins with K, she was not exempt, we came up with Ke'Lani (keh-lah-nee). The boy's middle names begin with A. So far, we've chosen Alexis.

Concerning the due date, I googled, "What month do you feel the first kick?" and the results were five months. So, I took it upon myself to estimate my own due date. But for future reference, Lean Not Unto Your Own Understanding!

> *Proverbs 3:5, 6 (NKJV): Trust in the Lord with all your heart, and lean not on your own understanding, in all your ways acknowledge Him, and He shall direct your paths.*

October 31, 2005

Nothing yet, I took another pregnancy test, number five. We found the couple that God wants us to bless to move into our house. I also had a baby shower at work today.

I can't remember what date I took pregnancy test number four, but the results for number five were—You guessed it, NEGATIVE!

By now, I am Full Force in Faith! I'm not worried about what anyone says or thinks, Doctors and All! I've told a good amount of people, including my students. As you read above, they surprisingly gave me a baby shower. They even had Ke'Lani's name on the cake. A few of them brought gifts, Wow! (Yes, my stomach had grown a bit with the round shape and all. But I was also a full-figured woman, so it wasn't that noticeable.)

November 8, 2005

We moved on Sunday, November 5, 2005. I've been having back pains only at night, it started November 3rd. I'm also having Braxton Hicks Contractions and a few people are telling me to go to the doctor.

I don't know what I'm going to do yet, just waiting (Struggling, Anxious).

> *Philippians 4:6 (NKJV): Be anxious for nothing, but in everything by prayer and supplication, with thanksgiving, let your requests be made known to God.*

November 17, 2005

I think I know what God meant when He said, *"You don't need a doctor."* Everyone is trying to make me go, but I'm waiting on instructions from God. I've been feeling back pains since last night, pressure down below, and leaking a clear fluid. It started at work around 4:15 PM. My co-workers have been really supportive.

November 18, 2005

So, I went into labor at work, in front of my students and other co-workers. Contractions were 2-4 minutes apart. My stomach was actually expanding and contracting. It was my aunt's birthday, and she was there getting her hair done. When she finished, she took me to the emergency room at University Hospital. The moment I walked into the emergency room and signed in; all the signs of labor STOPPED! I mean—Ceased and Disappeared!

They put me in a waiting area. The doctor came in to check me, pressed on my stomach, but felt NO BABY. They performed a pelvic exam, confirming only the excess fluid but NOTHING ELSE. I was there for approximately three hours until they released me to go home.

Once I got back to my car, I picked up Vonaye and Shawn and took them to my house to tell them what happened. They had been trying to call to tell me NOT to go to the doctor! I told them what happened when I got there and Vonaye began to cry.

Shawn said, "NO, NO, we can't stop believing! GOD would not show us ALL of that for Nothing!"

So we talked, cried, and stayed up late watching Trinity Broadcasting Network (TBN). Bishop Evans was discussing Faith and Distractions! At that point, Vonaye and I realized Shawn was right!

That day, as I recalled, was the WORST day of my life. I remembered a dream I had about me walking with people very close to me, and I had been shot in my side. Walking around with them, I was wounded and bleeding but not dying. No one knew or understood the process that God was taking me through, Not Even Me! A lot of logical reasoning and overthinking came into play. BUT GOD still had a plan that I had to walk out and see it through, to The End!

> *Jeremiah 29:11 (NIV): "For I know the plans I have for you," declares the Lord, "plans to prosper and not to harm you, plans to give you hope and a future." One version says, "to give you an Expected End."*

November 19, 2005

Vonaye, Shawn, and I praised God the majority of the day, listening to worship music. I also received more confirmation, watching TBN (Bishop Jakes and Bishop Long—Dream Killers)

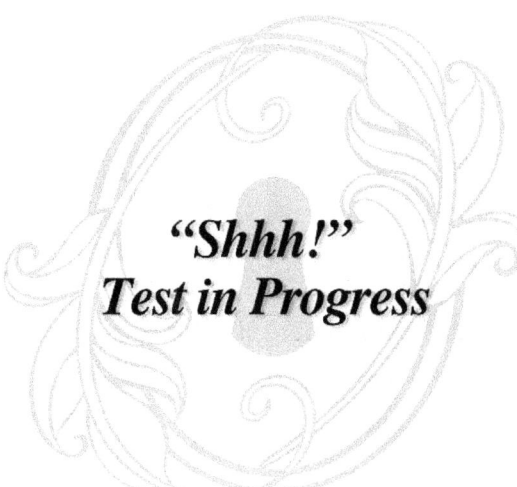

"Shhh!" Test in Progress

November 20, 2005

Sunday: Didn't go to church today (first time in a long time). I praised God at home, more Rhema Word/Prophetic Word:

"The Teacher doesn't talk while the Student takes the Test!"

As a teacher myself, I always make sure that I've taught my students what they need to know before administering a test on a particular subject. Every "Great Teacher" does. Now we are talking about "The Master Teacher." God has given me the necessary tools and materials I needed to pass this test. At times I felt as if He wasn't there because I didn't hear Him. He became silent! God had already prepared me through the Dreams, Visions, Word, and everything else He had shown me. So, there was no need for Him to speak at this time. My Faith HAD to be Tested and Tried—and that, It Was!

November 22, 2005

I stayed home, Kameron and Keelan went to Statesboro with Tony's parents, once he got home from work. For the past two days, I've prayed and cried just about all day! I even asked God, "When can I come off of this cross?"

The number 22 came up in my spirit for some reason. Tony was on his way out the door when a few family members showed up at our house. They talked to me first and then to Tony and me, together. They told me that God would give us a child if we both were in agreement, shared some scriptures with me, and told me to focus on the spiritual side of things. They also said I was going to reach people on a large scale, as Peter did.

I believe today, the number 22 represented Psalm 22. I am going to put a portion of the Chapter right here, because I believe this is for someone who feels you are alone, which is exactly how I felt.

YOU ARE NOT ALONE! GOD IS RIGHT THERE WITH YOU! DON'T MISTAKE HIS SILENCE FOR ABSENCE!
JUST TRUST HIM!

Psalm 22:1-11 (NKJV): My God, My God, why have You forsaken me? Why are You so far from helping me, and from the words of my groaning? O My God, I cry in the daytime, but You do not hear, and in the night season, and am not silent.

But You are holy, Enthroned in the praises of Israel. Our

> *fathers trusted in You. They trusted, and You delivered them. They cried to You, and were delivered. They trusted in You, and were not ashamed. But I am a worm, and no man, A reproach of men, and despised by the people. All those who see me ridicule me.*
>
> *They shoot out the lip, they shake the head, saying, "He trusted in the Lord, let Him rescue him, Let Him deliver him, since he delights in Him!" But You are He who took Me out of the womb, You made me trust while on my mother's breasts. I was cast upon You from birth. From my mother's womb You have been my God. Be not far from me, For trouble is near, For there is none to help.*

I felt as if I were all alone in a cold world, where no one felt my pain and agony. Some of my family was as supportive as they could be, but once again, no one really understood what I was going through, not even me! Surely nothing like this has ever happened before.

Actually, one topic Dr. Bynum spoke about at the summit was, "Let God Give You Something That's Never Happened Before." The closest thing that I could think of was with Mary, the mother of Jesus, which was not even close or comparable. But I now have an idea of how she felt with people thinking she was crazy, out of her mind, or lying!

November 23, 2005

Two of my co-workers stopped by the house today. I searched the scriptures concerning the Shunammite Woman, her constant response was, "IT IS WELL." The size of my stomach has gone down some. It was about the size of someone five months pregnant, no larger. Milk is discharging from my breasts: Enough to pump a few bottles!

November 24, 2005

Thanksgiving Day: Getting ready to go to Statesboro, I told Tony that God knows his heart better than he does. He asked me if I didn't think he knew his own heart. I told him, yes, but God knows it better. About two minutes later, he came to me and told me, when he was a teenager, he used to pray for a daughter with "pretty hair." But when he got older and started going to church more, he decided he'd be thankful for whatever God gave him because he only wanted one child. (He had a vasectomy after Keelan.) This showed me that he did have a desire for a little girl. I did at one time too, but it was not a major necessity. As I said before, I was perfectly fine with our two boys.

November 25, 2005

I don't know what I'm going to do about going back to work Monday, I was on Thanksgiving Break. I don't know what to tell my supervisor or the students. Please Help God!

November 28, 2005

I went back to work and told the students that I was having complications and I didn't want to talk about it. I told my supervisor that I was returning to work until further notice. The substitute teacher had already signed a contract to cover for me. This was my first day back, and it was a little awkward, but by the Grace of God, I made it through it!

PART 1 *The Journal* | A SEASON OF BIRTHING: *"Shhh!"* Test in Progress

November 29, 2005

My second day back at work, I was feeling really down. I sat behind my desk all day because my stomach has gone down and I've lost weight. Lee, a Pastor and old student of ours, stopped by unexpectedly. He said he had a feeling that he needed to stop by. We went outside to his truck and talked for about an hour and a half. His directions to me were to "Repent, Praise, and Pray," write down all the dreams I've had, erase the negative tape in my mind and replay the prophecies. (Still leaking fluid and still feeling kicks.)

November 30, 2005

Started out having a wonderful day. Everything was getting back to normal with my students and co-workers. I even got up from my desk and walked around, not ashamed. THEN, all of a sudden, my supervisor came to check on me. She looked at my stomach and started drilling me with questions about who my doctor was, what was said, when was my due date, and did I have an ultrasound? I felt SO Uncomfortable, and it really messed up the rest of my day!

I cried, telling God that I couldn't take this anymore, that I don't want to go through this! I feel like I've been lying to people. And as the scripture said, in my car as I was leaving the doctor's office, I felt that I had been DECEIVED, and that God may not show up! But now I'm going to erase the Negative Tape and Replay The Prophecies! November 2005—Worst Month of My Life!

And to think, this was only the beginning of the process I had to go through. I had a choice and free will to give up, if I wanted to. But there was NO WAY I was going to give up, no matter how hard, tough, or painful the process was going to be. Did I understand what I was going through and why, at this point? NO, I didn't. But I knew I had to TRUST GOD! And if I were going to continue the process, I knew I had to go all the way through it, to the END!

Philippians 1:6 (NKJV): Being confident of this very thing, that He who has begun a good work in you will complete it until the day of Jesus Christ.

Hebrews 12:2 (NKJV): Looking unto Jesus, the author and finisher of our faith, who for the joy that was set before Him endured the cross, despising the shame, and has sat down at the right hand of the throne of God.

December 1, 2005

My supervisor sent an email to tell me she wanted to see me in her office whenever I got a chance. I thought maybe she'd tried to call my doctor or something. I was nervous all day about what she might ask or say. It ended up being nothing major, she was just being nosey. She told me that the payroll department needed documentation from my doctor stating how long I was going to be out of work and when (second time asking). Well, I'd already talked to the department manager a few days ago, and she told me I could bring in documentation after having the baby.

*Miracles come through your greatest pain!

No Smooth Sailing

December 4, 2005

Everyone is asking me when I will have the baby. I have no answer for them. My stomach looks like it comes and goes according to my environment. I'm feeling very little movement, thumping every now and then. Walking by Faith sometimes requires you to do things that you don't understand. Obey what you don't understand, Spirit led, of course.

2 Corinthians 5:7 (NKJV): For we walk by faith, not by sight.

I heard John Hagee say: "He didn't promise smooth sailing, but He promised you a safe landing," and "Miracles still happen."

I had a dream before all this started, about an airplane taking off, leveling, and then running out of gas. The plane started descending in a nosedive fashion; however, we were enjoying the view from the window on the way down. We landed in a beautiful body of crystal blue water! Tony and I both were passengers on the plane.

Bishop Jakes said, "What God wants to give you, may defy all human logic."

*Though He slay me, yet will I trust Him. Now, I can relate to Job, Joseph, Mary, and Abraham.

December 8, 2005

I've been seeing a lot of messages on TBN (Trinity Broadcasting Network) about storms. I had a dream of being surrounded by tornados and avoiding them by going in the opposite direction. But in order to get to the other side, I have to go through the storm. I turned the TV to TBN and there was a movie playing. The first thing I saw was Jesus asleep in the boat while the storm was raging. Lord, I pray You give me peace in the midst of the storm that I'm about to encounter, in order to get to the other side!

December 11, 2005

Sunday Morning, 6 AM: (Anyone who knows me knows that waking up that early is not a common practice of mine.) I woke up to TBN with John Francis talking about cursing the enemy so he would not get you to abort the dream God put in you. Rod Parsley spoke next about 'Fear or Faith.' A double minded man is unstable in all his ways, according to James 1:8. So I got up out of the bed, went to the spare bedroom and prayed. I told God that I believed and from that moment on, no matter what I felt or didn't feel, I was not going to waver between two opinions any longer. I went to church a few hours later, and the message was about Abraham's test of faith from Genesis Chapter 22. After the service, the pastor called me into the office and asked if I was ready to preach my first message. I replied with a "Yes Sir."

(I'm still leaking fluid.) Oh, I forgot my aunt gave a corporate prophecy at church: "God is working on supernatural provisions for you. He is changing your situation around in the heavens. Don't give up!"

December 13, 2005

At work around 9:30 AM, I went to the restroom and my underwear was soaked. The fluid leaking has increased again! It leaked heavily all day. I also showed my co-workers the milk coming from my breasts.

December 15, 2005

Thursday, Campus Wide Christmas Dinner: Everyone was there, faculty and staff. One lady asked if I was back already, she thought I'd had the baby. Everyone keeps asking me, "How much longer?"

Back in the office, my supervisor called accidentally, trying to reach another department, but started questioning me again about my due date. She asked if I had turned any documentation in to payroll yet, and I told her they said I could bring it in after delivery. She then proceeds to tell me she was told that I needed it beforehand. Well, I have been drilled and felt somewhat harassed by her a couple of times and I'm trying to keep my composure!

December 16, 2005

Bishop Jakes was on TV this morning discussing, not reacting to the attack because the battle is not yours! God sees what you're going through. I went to work and had no plans of going to the Business Division Christmas Party, but I went in spite of what everyone has been saying about me. My supervisor ended up sitting next to me at the table. I also felt led to present to her the gift that was from everyone, and I did.

December 25, 2005

I couldn't sleep last night. I was hoping and expecting Ke'Lani to come, and when it didn't happen, I was very disappointed. I began to feel deceived again. It was a rough day, but I pressed my way through it. I stayed to myself at both family gatherings, not talking to anyone.

December 26, 2005

I've been feeling like it's too late to happen. Mark Chironna preached a message: "If It Wants to Happen, It Needs To Be Spoken." He talked about Seven Favor Blockers:

1. You feel it's too late
2. You feel like you don't have what it takes
3. You believe you are unproductive
4. You believe it's too good to be true
5. You believe your prayers don't make a difference
6. You feel ashamed of where you are and where you've been

7. You feel like it's impossible

(I'm also concerned about going back to work after the holiday break.)

This is how I felt on so many levels! Definitely the feeling of impossibility came over me. But the Bible says in Mark 9:23 (NKJV), Jesus said to him, "If you can believe, all things are possible to him who believes."

It's as if step by step, God had messages for me even when He himself wasn't speaking to me directly. So, when you think He's silent, pay attention to what He's saying through other sources. And remember Deuteronomy 31:6 (NKJV), "Be strong and of good courage, do not fear nor be afraid of them, for the Lord your God, He is the one who goes with you. He will not leave you nor forsake you."

January 7, 2006

I haven't written in a while (about two weeks) because I made up my mind that I had to move on. Not forgetting about what God is going to do, but just not worrying and having anxiety about it. I'm seeking a place of peace. Since the last time I wrote, I've cried out to God and been up and down emotionally. I was even hoping she'd come on January 1, which was seven months from July 1, last year when everything started.

I went back to work and told a few people who asked that I lost the baby. I told my supervisor the doctor saw no baby but has no explanation for what I'm going through. My students haven't said anything to me, respecting my privacy. One student shared her testimony with me, and I now understand why God used her to encourage me on several occasions.

My co-worker Angela (who is like a big sister) and I are talking more now. I explained to her that I'm going through a spiritual process. I understand that God has me on my "Island of Patmos" as He did John the Revelator, isolated for a reason. He is preparing me for ministry and something great!

January 14, 2006

I still believe God is going to send Ke'Lani, but I don't know when. I am still feeling kicking, milk from my breasts, and fluid leaking. I am starting to understand "Destiny Processing." I am entering into my "Rest" of faith. I talked to my mom about where I am right now, that it hasn't stopped or gone away.

The pastor preached a message last Sunday about not having to understand everything God is doing: Joseph had to tell his dreams, in order for the plan to be fulfilled (Genesis 37). Yes, people are still talking about me. However, I'm trying to move on with my life. I also finally got a chance to tell Tony how I've been feeling.

January 22, 2006

Preached my first message Friday night, January 20. My topic was, "You Shall Live." I spoke from Ezekiel 37, The Valley of Dry Bones. I didn't know what to expect, but I felt good about it. Everyone said I did well. I wasn't even nervous.

Catch the Wind

January 31, 2006

Tuesday: Someone I met at work, shared testimonies with me. She is from Africa and has experienced God's miraculous power. She invited me to her home, prayed with me, and invited me to her place of worship. I went looking for the building on Wednesday night but couldn't find it.

February 8, 2006

I found the building and finally went to bible study after being invited. Afterwards, I went up for prophecy and several people prophesied to me. The First Lady of the house said to me, "This is your year of favor. You've been through unnecessary battles and the enemy kept beating you up. You need more faith in this season and then you'll see manifestation of what God has promised."

The pastor told me that God was settling some issues on my behalf. He also said that I would become a businesswoman in the community.

This was the first time anyone had spoken directly to me concerning this situation. Yes, I heard messages from ministers on television, but this was more personal. And the awesome thing about it was, she didn't know me and had never even seen me before, and God used her to speak to me. At that moment, I felt that His silence was now broken.

February 19, 2006

Sunday: Went to the 8 AM service. The message was about Faith and Prophecy, God doesn't show up the way we expect, and don't try to make it happen, wait on God. The pastor spoke to Tony about the call of God on his life. He also stirred up the gift in me by the laying on of hands (2 Timothy 1:6). God led us to leave the church we attended for eight years to join this ministry.

1 Thessalonians 5:20-21 (VOICE): Don't downplay prophecies. Take a close look at everything, test it, then cling to what is good.

March 7, 2006

I talked to Teresa and told her everything I'd been going through. I had a season of dreams May—June 2006: Gated Subdivision, Quit my job at the college, Giant Bank Robber and Thief arrested.

Mark Chironna spoke about Gilgal: full circle, when you get to that point you either breakdown or breakthrough! I've come full circle and I'm at a breakpoint. I'm going to break through!

PART 1 *The Journal* | A SEASON OF BIRTHING: *Catch The Wind*

June 27, 2006

So much has happened since the last time I've written. June 18th was Father's Day. Tony ministered at CTW. The title was, "Today We Have Become Fathers." He gave his testimony about his relationship with his father. He called his father up and apologized for anything he'd ever done. Almost everyone was in tears.

Our lights were cut off, because we missed the payment deadline. I went to pay the light bill (we had the money for it) and they told me if I had come yesterday, they wouldn't have cut them off. They were out from 2 PM until 12:45 PM the next day.

June 28, 2006

Last night was very unique. It was mid-summer and very hot in the house without electricity. We had candles lit all over the house, including in the bathrooms. I had a dream about a bank robber who looked like a giant. But he was arrested, and we were told that he wouldn't rob anyone else, anymore. I read my bible, with the candles still lit and came upon these scriptures:

> *Exodus 14:13 (NKJV): And Moses said to the people, "Do not be afraid. Stand still and see the salvation of the Lord, which He will accomplish for you today. For the Egyptians whom you see today, you shall see again no more forever..."*

> *Exodus 12:42 (NIV): Because the Lord kept vigil that night to bring them out of Egypt, on this night all the Israelites are to keep vigil to honor the Lord for the generations to come.*

A few months ago, a prophet told us, Tony needs to anoint my stomach and pray because there is a little girl coming (second confirmation) and don't be surprised if it's twins. Well, God is showing me, bit by bit, the pieces of this puzzle through revelations. When it all started, the baby was the only focus, then a vision for a major business was revealed.

So, I began to think that I was birthing the business and the baby would be the reward on the latter end. This vision is a part of the "Kingdom Millionaire" prophecy that was spoken last year by Dr. Cindy Trimm. So, the twins could possibly represent the baby and the business.

July 18, 2006

We still ride around looking at houses and land regularly. I saw a beautiful three-story house online, so I asked Lee (who was also a realtor) about it. The house is in Mount Vintage Plantation in South Carolina. We went to see it, the door was unlocked, so we walked in and looked around. I fell in love with it! Balconies on the back, theater room, step down great room, the works! It's not completely finished yet. We ride over there very often (faith building).

July 19, 2006

Wednesday Night: An Apostle came from Atlanta to minister. He told me, "Woman of God, there is healing for your body. In your fallopian tube area, I see a miracle! I see a baby, and you're not going to need surgery! A miracle is about to take place!" (Third Confirmation)

There is a tingling feeling that goes up my spine that feels exactly like an epidural. I'm ready, God! You haven't forgotten me! The Apostle told Tony, "And it ain't dead, Fred!" (Referring to the vasectomy)

October 5, 2006

So much is happening. Everything is beginning to make sense now. On October 3rd, God showed me a portion of our assignment in ministry. It is to help people discover and fulfill their purpose and destiny in the kingdom. Our areas of anointing are faith, prosperity, and miracles. We are literally walking in our season. We sowed a seed for Atonement. Expecting a harvest, Ke'Lani next month and our house will be ready in December. God does speak to you concerning times and seasons: *The Spirit knows all things and dwells in us!*

I can't wait to see our baby girl, Ke'Lani Alexis Moore. God, you really haven't forgotten!

November 9, 2006

Tony and I have really been through some trials in our marriage within the last three weeks. I had a dream about tornados and him in the passenger seat of his truck. I know a lot of the spiritual warfare is because of what's about to happen.

The back labor started again tonight. I feel a tingling all the way from the bottom of my spine to the top. It's like a supernatural epidural, and the fluid is leaking again! I need to get my house in order and prepare for what is about to happen. I have so many questions: God, how will she look? How big or small will she be? I think I'm going to change her middle name from Alexis to Amiracle, but I have to talk to Tony. Ke'Lani Amiracle Moore.

November 16, 2006

Time has really gone by fast. Only two more days! My back is hurting, increased fluid, and stomach tightening up. We know that our breakthrough is coming through this miracle.

UNVEILING DESTINY
Don't You Drown That Baby

December 5, 2006

November 18 has come and gone. Ke'Lani did not come on that day. I waited around all day, even up until midnight. I now remember telling God that I didn't want her to come on that day because it was the worst day of my life last year. Now I understand why it hasn't happened.

A few mornings ago, God woke Tony and me up around 2:30 AM. We both stayed up for a while. I couldn't go back to sleep, so I turned the TV up to watch TBN. It was 4:30 AM, Mark Chironna was speaking about Winter Seasons and how everything in your life looks dead and hopeless. But it's in those seasons when God does the greatest miracles! He discussed Mary and Elizabeth's relation to each other and how they both were expecting babies. Elizabeth hadn't felt her baby move, although she was in her sixth month. She tried to conceive most of her life, but nothing ever happened for her. She felt like the poem by Langston Hughes that says:

"When dreams die, life is a broken-winged bird that cannot fly, and when dreams go, life is a field frozen with snow."

When Mary greets Elizabeth, the baby in her womb leaped for the first time. He also said, "You are about to get a visitor and a prophetic word of release. The reason for the delay in the thing you've been carrying is because it hasn't been connected with its purpose and reason for existence. But this Christmas Season you're about to be greeted by an angel/prophetic messenger."

WOW! Well, the following night, I had two dreams! Pay close attention and you'll see exactly what He said unfold!

The Dreams and Interpretation: My family and I were at my parent's old house (the one I grew up in). Shawn and I walked outside, looked up in the sky and saw a big ball of fire shoot down from heaven and land in a field behind the house. Smoke filled the area and spread all over the city. We ran into the house to tell everyone what we saw. We thought we were being bombed by another country. Then we told everyone that we needed to evacuate. What seemed like my parent's old house then turned into our house. I remember packing a few important items. It was daylight when the fireball hit, but by the time we finished evacuating, it was evening. I remember going back in the house to find my journal after putting the boys in the car.

Later that same night in another dream: I was walking in a neighborhood with large houses. I saw one house with furniture outside and another house that was turned into a studio. I saw the name of the studio written on the house, but I don't remember what it was. I saw TVs all over the studio. I walked down past the house and ran into a guy. I asked him, "Do you remember me?"

"Yes, I know who you are," he said. We talked for a moment. I had my journal in my hand and he said, "Is that your journal? Can I read it?" He started reading it and said, "Wow! This is really good!" He had on a hat and glasses and looked like a producer or director.

The same night (no longer dreaming), a couple who were friends of ours from church, came over after dinner. I showed the wife the recording of Mark Chironna's message about the prophetic messenger coming to visit. I then told her about the dream concerning the ball of fire. She had the same interpretation as we did. The fireball from heaven was the birth. She began to go into more detail with the interpretation: "The smoke spreading around the city was the testimony of the miracle."

Chironna also said there wouldn't have been a need for a John the Baptist if there wasn't a Jesus. But John's birth and reason for existence was to proclaim the coming of The Lord Jesus Christ. As she and I kept talking she said, "The birth will proclaim the Glory of God. Her purpose and reason for existence has been revealed! She will have a John the Baptist anointing (minus the beheading). A Prophetess to the Nations, she will be."

My friend was the messenger that came to reveal Ke'Lani's purpose. That's why there has been such a delay in the process. Why birth something and not know why you are birthing it? Why go through a twenty-two-month process and not know why you had to go through it?

October 1, 2007

The last time I've written in this journal was December 5, 2006. So much has happened over this ten-month period. Tony and I will have a ministry by the name of "Unveiling Destiny Global Ministries," along with several businesses. So much has been birthed through this process of destiny. Around the beginning of August 2007, God gave me a dream and began dealing with Tony and I, about our season being up at CTW. We went back to our home church.

Well once again, for the third time, we're approaching the season that I go into labor. During this season, God has given instructions through my husband that I am not to discuss anything with anyone outside of our household. I have learned so much through this process and I thank God for all we've been through, even the financial difficulties. This process started back in July 2005, and for 28 months, I've felt our daughter kicking in my stomach every day. I haven't been to the doctor since November 18, 2005.

October 16, 2007

We moved out of the house that we were renting, into a Townhouse on June 8, 2007. The address was 2240. God gave Teresa bits and pieces of information on both houses that we moved in.

1 Corinthians 13:9 (NLT): Now our knowledge is partial and incomplete, and even the gift of prophecy reveals only part of the whole picture!

October 27, 2007

The fluid leaking has started again and is beginning to increase. Okay God, I'm really, really, really ready! FAITH is the Key that Unlocks the Door! So many lives and people will be touched by Your miracle, God! I've learned so much that I can't begin to write it all (just yet)! Lord Jesus, I Love You and You are Worthy of All the Glory!

October 29, 2007

Last month, I made the biggest decision I've ever had to make in my entire life! I left my job of almost 7 years! I stepped out on faith by the leading of the Holy Spirit. No one understood my decision, not even me! I planned on retiring from there by the age of fifty-two. But God had to get me out of my comfort zone and push me into the Faith Zone because of where He is taking me. (Fluid seems to leak more around late afternoon and evening.)

October 31, 2007

Back pains started around 9:30 PM yesterday. I just started praising God through song and dance.

November 13, 2007

A minister was on TBN and the message was as follows: "God has an appointment, a set time, and He is about to manifest your miracle. Your bedroom is about to be turned into a Labor and Delivery Room! The reason you've gone through what you have, is because God is positioning you! It's a fixed appointment for you to bring forth a new order of God's presence in the earth. You're not just birthing Samuel, Hannah. Things may start in Chaos but end up in Cosmos (which is orderly and harmonious)! Even when situations begin in chaos, they end exactly the way He promised. This is the greatest season of glory. God will be glorified. Only that which is permanent can go into this new season with you. People are going to scratch their heads and say,

'Not only did God do what He said but, He did above it!' And that business is going to fund the Kingdom of God and your children will call you blessed."

God's ways are not our ways, neither are His thoughts our thoughts (Isaiah 55:8). Praise comes through experience. Opposition and Adversity is Opportunity! Real Praise is Personal, Private, and Intimate. Public Praise is sometimes done out of Protocol and not always Passion.

Not only was I birthing the PROMISE, but also the PLAN of God: Ministry and Business. God will not allow us to produce anything that's contaminated, so He takes us through the PROCESS to get all impurities out!

Ever since I discovered the call of God for my life, there has always been someone with a prophetic gift around me. In this season, it is Jessica, a friend of mine.

(Fluid leaking and back hurting: five days away from the greatest days of our lives. I Love You Jesus!)

November 15, 2007

I watched a show called "Amazing Baby Deliveries" where one lady, who didn't know she was pregnant, had twins in the car. Another lady was a teacher who didn't know either, and she had the baby in class. I felt the need to prepare (extra cleaning at the house, etc.). I have a bag that's been packed since 2005 with baby things and things I would need at the hospital.

Angela called to check on me, she asked what was going on with me. I told her nothing, well nothing bad, but spiritual. So, I went by the school to get my hair done and show my face, so she'd know I was fine.

November 17, 2007

I woke up at 9:50 AM with back pains. They have become a bit more intense.

Later that evening at 6:10 PM: I went shopping for my three men. I've been alone all day, alone with God, and I've really enjoyed it. When I went inside Shoe Carnival, my back started hurting even more. So, I left and headed home. Once I got home, I began thanking, praising, worshipping, decreeing, declaring, binding, and loosing. I had an awesome time with The Lord (Private Praise)! I really felt some things being released from the heavens by the angels. I thanked God for everything I'd gone through, from the persecution, lies, being laughed at, criticized, thought to be crazy, you name it. I thank You God for what is about to happen!

November 20, 2007

Wow! I have learned so much in the past 48 hours! On the night of November 18th, I spent the entire day waiting patiently, so I thought. I got up and prayed around 11:50 AM. Around 10:30 PM I Prayed and Cried, Screamed and Hollered, Decreed and Declared, Spoke about NOW Faith, Mountain Moving Faith, and Healing Faith, to the point that I would Not Faint, Give Up, Take No for an Answer or Give In! I was going to Take It By Force—but there was one small problem—She didn't come once again, for the third time.

Yesterday, after I took the boys to school, I broke down crying in the car, wondering what happened. Why did this happen to me again?

Where is the promise? Three is the number of completion and resurrection, right? I still had back pains that had not gone away. Vonaye called me around lunchtime, around 3 PM, and asked if everything was ok. I felt something inside me telling me to go ahead (song). Don't shake it this time! Don't wait another year, looking for her to come on a specific date. If you think it's going to happen on a certain date, then you'll keep going around that same mountain year after year! Are you concerned about the date or the promise? I had to realize that God doesn't need my help to perform this miracle, just my faith. The faith was there, but my help was in the way!

I do know this: This is the SEASON for the promise, and that's all I need to know! But I am not going to let it go this time, as I have in the past, waiting on a date to come around again. This time, I am not going to limit God to a date or time frame. He knows when He wants it to take place. I just need to be in expectation, but while RESTING! This time I will take it by force with my faith and not give up! I now see how going through and learning through the process increases your anointing! This time, I'm coming out with a fight and not waiting another year! NOW FAITH! God is not going to allow man to get the glory out of this miracle. If it were to happen on the exact date that I estimated, it would've been as though I had a part in bringing it to pass. God has a way of teaching us a lesson while still providing Mercy and Grace to give us another chance to get it right! Thank You Jesus!

December 31, 2007

I had a very significant dream last night! Before I went to bed, I prayed, "Lord, I don't want to go into another year holding on to anything that I need to let go of! If I need to let this go, please show me so that I can start the New Year fresh!"

Well, in the dream I was in a large swimming pool holding a baby in my arms. I was trying to walk from one side of the pool to the stairs to exit. All of a sudden, large ocean-like waves started surging in the pool. I then had to change the way I was carrying the baby, from my side to holding the baby with one hand, elevated high in the air. My mother was standing at the edge of the pool, near the stairs, saying, "Don't You Drown That Baby!"

I knew then that this process was still not over. I had to continue on! I'd come too far to turn around, give up, or quit!

Summary of 2008-2010

In January 2008, we attended a family member's ministry. In the six months that we were there, I taught Sunday School. "The Fruit of the Spirit" was the main focus. Well, to my surprise, God had me teach on LOVE for the entire six months! Little did I know, it was for a reason. My Love was about to be extensively tested.

We moved to Macon by the leading of Holy Spirit in July 2008, and we knew it was for a season. Although we liked living in Macon, Tony didn't like his job there. So, after six months, he went back to his old job, mainly staying there with a co-worker and visiting us periodically. This was a major transition for our family as we stayed in Macon for one year.

November 18, 2008

The church we attended was invited to attend a TBN live taping in Atlanta. Tony and I, along with my longtime friend Sonya, and the pastors rode together. During praise and worship, out of nowhere I began to feel intense back pains and fluid leaking, excessively! I went into the studio restroom and my underwear was soaked! On the ride back home, I felt major pressure in my cervical area! I kept trying to hide what was going on. I was riding in the back seat and Tony was driving. When we arrived home, I went to the bathroom, and the pressure kept getting stronger! At around 11:50 PM, I felt the urge to PUSH! So, I pushed and pushed, but nothing would come out. My cervix had even opened up at least five centimeters, if not more! I didn't want to say anything to Tony, so I just prayed and cried out to God, and it eventually stopped after midnight.

I remember going to a doctor in February 2009, while still in Macon. I even had another ultrasound, which revealed nothing! The female doctor said to me, in a very rude tone, "Even elephants deliver after two years!"

There I was, sharing a little of what I had been experiencing in my body over the past three years, and she was very insensitive to my situation. That was the first time I had gone to a doctor since 2005, and that was the type of treatment I experienced!

May 4, 2009

Wow! Time is really moving. It has been almost one year and a half since I last wrote, and almost four years since this journey began. So much has transpired since then. Of course, my Faith has increased! I'm finally at the point where I don't care what anyone's opinion is about my situation!

Prophecy: Speedy recovery, no matter what it looks like. The shield of faith has kept you protected from the enemy and his attacks. There is a miracle in your womb. Apologies will come from those close to you. Teach My Word!

Several random people have asked me if I want more children or a little girl. My response is always, "Only if it's God's Will!"

We moved back to my hometown. The boys and I stayed at my parent's house for about one and a half years, with Tony there off and on. My mom and I went to Atlanta to have a consultation with a Wholistic Healing Doctor whom I told about my situation, but to no surprise, she didn't have much to say. However, when I put my feet in the Detox-Foot Bath, based on the color of the water, it revealed that there was something going on with my reproductive organs—Hmm?

November 2009 and 2010

These two years were very similar. Very little kicking, fluid leaking, and labor signs occurred—Yes, they still occurred. I really believe that my faith was weaker in those times. I had really decided to move on with my life and not focus on the promise. Even more problems began to arise between Tony and me.

Peace! Be Still!

February 2011

We purchased a house and moved in early February. We had a beautiful house, but home was far from its identity. The problems in our marriage intensified. The arguing, not seeing eye to eye, not agreeing on hardly anything, our marriage was under full attack!

September 8, 2011

Prophecy: I have chosen you to carry my Miracle Baby: Someone else refused to do it!

This confirms that God will replace you if you don't fulfill your assignment. King Saul was a prime example, replaced by King David. Also, Joshua and Caleb both fulfilled the assignment that Moses was supposed to fulfill.

Don't get replaced. Surrender to His Perfect Will for your life!

I had a dream about a baby stuck in the oven. The light inside was on, but the oven was not. Tony was standing there looking with me. He said, "At least the oven isn't on." The baby was on the bottom rack. All of a sudden, I reached in and pulled the baby out "by the head." (The last statement has significant meaning and will be discussed later in the book.)

October 9, 2011

The last time I actually journaled was in May 2009. Let's see, where do I begin? I taught a message at FTCM, which we've been attending since 2010. The title was, "What Are You Carrying" and "Are You Ready To Deliver?" I had a dream the night before and for the first time, I saw her in a full, complete view! I could say a lot right now, but I will sum it up in one word, in a minute. I read a book that my friend Olaundra gave me titled, "Purpose Conceived," and another book by Smith Wigglesworth, "Do The Impossible!"

When we moved into our new house, back in February, I actually hung up the baby clothes that I was given at the shower in 2005, in the spare bedroom closet. This is the description of the state I'm in right now: Sum = PEACE! No worries and learning to trust God even more.

October 18, 2011

Sometime in June or July, I heard a message that Joel Osteen preached about believing God will do what He promised. He actually said, "It's going to happen this year!" Well, of course, that sparked something in me.

In late August, I'd made up my mind that I'd been through too much to just come out of this process with an ordinary "Natural Birth." This WILL be a "Miraculous Supernatural Birth!"

November 15, 2011

Watching Mark Chironna on television. He was talking about dealing with fear. So, I asked myself what I was afraid of. I had a fear of "dis-appointment," especially concerning my husband and our boys. So many years had gone by, but no manifestation had taken place and I didn't want to let them down. Now I'm going to deal with the fear and "I will not miss my appointment!"

Sunday morning, as soon as I turned on the TV, Joel Osteen said, "Joshua marched around the walls of Jericho, seven times! Praise puts you in the birth position to receive the promise!"

I've been listening to J.J. Hairston and Youthful Praise "Hear Me Lord." This part in particular stands out:

Every… miracle… In your Word

Is preceded by a sound

There's always a great sound.

I'm not waiting for anything else

To make a sound for me

I need a miracle

So I'll make my own sound right now!

The hardest part of transition is coming out of it! We've made it out of transition. Visited CTW on October 31, 2011. The prophet that was ministering was someone I'd never met before and he called me out, which happens often when I visit prophetic ministries.

Prophecy: A huge door just swung open for you, major

opportunities and financial blessings! Money is overtaking you! A move is also coming, I see a house with furniture already in it.

That was the third time I'd heard about a house with the furniture already in it.

November 16, 2011

There was severe weather on my way home from work. I went by and picked up the boys from my parent's house. I received a call from one of my aunts asking where we were. She thought I was going to stay at my parents' for a little while, as I normally would. I told her that we were almost home. As I turned in our driveway, the sky was black, and the clouds were very dark. The wind was howling, and the lightning was piercing as it struck everything in its path! She called back and said that a TORNADO was spotted in the clouds in Shell Bluff, which is about three miles up the road from us!

Once we were in the house, I began to pray in the Spirit, rebuking the wind and commanding it to go. I was engaging in serious Spiritual Warfare! At one point, I went outside and spoke to the wind and pointed in the direction that it needed to go. The wind got so strong and fierce that dirt and debris were flying everywhere! The boys were watching and praying to themselves. We turned the television on to the news channel and they were showing where the tornado was located on the radar. The wind was registered at 8.1 in strength. Amazed, we watched as the tornado moved on the radar in the direction I pointed! Then, all of a sudden, the storm ceased.

Tony walked in the house from work about two hours later and told us that the tornado touched down in Shell Bluff. So, we all got in the car and took a ride up the road to look at the damage it caused. As we left our driveway, only three houses up from ours, trees and limbs were blown down. But a few miles up the road, trees were uprooted, the door of a storage building was blown off, and even the siding from a house and a small trailer were blown across the street into a field!

Interpretation: Power—Protection—Promise. My praise and intercession were the bomb that set off the grenade, which released three sets of legions of angels! When I saw the strong wind in my front yard, it was the angels pushing back the storm. There were also two large angels (taller than the house) guarding the house. One on the left corner and Gabriel on the right corner of the house, with their two swords crossing over the house forming an X. Power, Protecting, the Promise!

The enemy is surely upset about what will take place and the impact it will have. The whole event reminded me of the dream with the bomb (grenade) in my parent's backyard.

December 31, 2011

Nothing Happened Again! Earlier this month, I went back to the original doctor's office from 2005, but to a different doctor earlier this month. This was the fourth time I'd been to a doctor, including the wholistic doctor. I told him about all the symptoms that I'd been experiencing over the years and around the same time each year. I didn't mention the spiritual aspects of the events. I had another ultrasound which once again revealed, NOTHING! The doctor mentioned that my uterus was enlarged. He scheduled me for a procedure that involved my colon and a scope. He thought that I possibly had some scarring in my intestines that was causing the kicking and moving symptoms. And for the record it revealed, nothing!

Prophetic 2012 & 2013

The year 2012 was very prophetic. God spoke to me through prophetic words constantly throughout the year. He spoke of "The Promise," Business, Ministry, and Family. These utterances from God helped keep me in a consistent state of faith! In these last few years of the trial, I HAD NO TIME TO DOUBT! ONLY BELIEVE!

> *1 Corinthians 14:3 (AMP): But [on the other hand] the one who prophesies speaks to people for edification [to promote their spiritual growth] and [speaks words of] encouragement [to uphold and advise them concerning the matters of God] and [speaks words of] consolation [to compassionately comfort them].*

March 25, 2012

Prophecy: Not Procreation but Manifestation, 'The Unborn Seed is for Tony.' Movie Productions: From Dreams to Destiny, California, Book Signing. Miracles are at your fingertips, financial overflow.

Open your mouth, don't need a prophet to confirm.

April 28, 2012

Prophecy: Divine Connections, Rivers are Flowing, TV Studio, Nourishing your faith like a plant: Gain and Increase without getting prideful, Soon! Genesis 8:22: Revelation of the measures. Business Arena, get ready! Airplane, Suits, TV Producer, "I reward those who are faithful!" Setting you up on high, it's your time to shine. Tony is not going anywhere: two peas in a pod.

November 19, 2012

I started feeling sick yesterday, so I stayed home from work today for the first time. I had severe stomach cramps, viral-like symptoms, and the chills. But to no surprise—Nothing happened again! Tony left home in July and returned yesterday. We have been separated a few times, this past year.

February 2013

Prophecy: New Doors, New Level, Heightened Sense of Security in God, The Promised Seed: I have not forgotten. Cut out the middleman with the house. Perpetual Blessing: Grandma's Land.

Before I pick up where I left off with the prophecies, let me say I have written in my journal every day consecutively since I started October 22, 2013. I made a vow that I would write every day until I had nothing else to write. I was getting sleepy around 11:30 PM and kept telling myself to get up and write. All of a sudden, Keelan came upstairs to our room and knocked on the door. Tony was asleep, so

Keelan whispered in a very eager to help voice, "Mom, wake up! Did you write? You've got to write!" He even had my journal in his hand. Needless to say, I got up and am writing now, thanks to our son!

April - June 2013

Prophecy: Jacksonville, Spiritual Wisdom Advisors, Crown with four corners as rubies representing: Royalty, Excellency, Wisdom, and Perfection. Miracle Teacher, Benefactors, Connect with those in Kingdom Authority. Not just a Teacher but an Institution, Global Destiny. Anointing of Establishment, Enlargement, and Empowerment: Growth, Carrying Your Cross, Crucial Timeframe—You Set the Bar and I'll Raise the Standard!

(You may not understand the prophecies, but they were given to me in the way I understood and also according to my faith. God always confirmed what He spoke as well. As He would also randomly place people in my path to confirm. Another key factor with prophecy is timing. Most of what was spoken in 2012 and 2013 didn't begin manifesting until 2019- 2021!)

July - August 2013

Prophecy: The answer is in the book! The Dream Book! The question is: Where is "The Riches and the Glory of His Inheritance in the Saints?" A lot will transpire in 7 years, by the age of 42. Completion of the cycles of 7! Opening of Tremendous Doors! The Lion and Lamb Revelation: Know when to be silent and when to speak boldly! Going up a Ladder Backwards, separate from the norm: Top of the Ladder: will get the Revelation of Why This Way—Through Suffering! Will give Revelation—Link into the Future! Joseph and

Job! School of Warfare for your Household! Last time saying, "I'm tired of doing the same thing." Mourning is Over: Time to Dance! 9th Month of 2014: Major Change from the Head—Down!

September 13, 2013

I scheduled our very first cruise for September 27-29, 2013. We were to sail on the Bahamas Celebration. Tony and I have still been having difficult times in our relationship. We are very much in need of a getaway, just the two of us: Especially since we never had an official honeymoon in our 14 years of marriage.

I was sitting at the front desk at work and one of my students, who I'd been ministering to, walked in and asked me a question about the bible. She'd been reading the bible! I was so happy and excited! After we finished talking, I ran into the restroom and began crying and weeping! I was excited about the student reading the Bible and at the same time saddened because my home was a wreck. I felt like I was effective in my assignment at work and with ministering to others, but my marriage was continuing to fall apart!

Prophecy: Taking you to 'Another Place,' As Paul, fighting the Good Fight and Not in Vain. As Zachariah, be silent in this season. Be Confident, Bold, Daring, Strong, and Courageous: Lift up your head! Extracting everything that needs to be, so it won't be detected and you will no longer be affected! The Cross with a Light: Every time you see Tony, remember Me and plead the Blood over him! I'm doing A Work in him. Spend more time with Me, get before Me and let Me pour into you: On the trip on the ship. Meeting Spot on the ship, White Garment with Jesus! You're Not Wasting Your Time.

September 26-29, 2013

A few days before leaving for the cruise, Tony started saying he didn't know if he was going. He said he didn't know if he was going to be able to get off work, even though he'd already requested it off. That may have somewhat been the case, but I believe he just didn't want to go. Why? Him and I, driving to Florida alone and staying on the ship for two days, meant no escape from conversation dealing with our issues and reconciling. I knew the enemy was in his ear because of the healing and deliverance it would bring to our marriage. But to no avail. I realized I was fighting a strong principality and power! Needless to say, He Didn't Go! He stayed home with the boys.

So, at the last minute, the morning of having to leave, I had to find someone to go with me. All of my friends were at work! I called Diane, a sister from our church, and she was able to go. However, I was very upset with my husband. Well, I was actually Furious! But I was also thankful that I didn't have to travel alone. I still managed to enjoy the trip and find peace in the midst of the chaos! There was a particular spot on the deck of the ship where we sat in the lounge chairs either early in the morning or late at night. Each time I came to that spot, I felt the Presence of God! I felt like Jesus was sitting right there with me (prophecy fulfilled)!

School of Warfare

September 29, 2013

On the way back from the cruise, we stopped by the church of a pastor who Diane knew in Jacksonville. During the altar call, to no surprise, he called me out.

Prophecy: Better is the end of a thing than the beginning there of (Ecclesiastes 7:8). What God has blessed, no man can curse! People are not expecting you to make it out this time, but God will get the Glory! "Woman of God, I see swords coming out of your mouth!"

This is when the Warfare Intensified!

October 2, 2013

I was off from work for seven days, so I prayed in the Spirit every day! I have been through fiery trials with the enemy attacking me through my husband and my own child! However, it has taught me how to war in the realm of the Spirit!

Ephesians 6:12 (NKJV): For we do not wrestle against flesh and blood (people), but against principalities, against powers, against the rulers of the darkness of this age, against spiritual hosts of wickedness in the heavenly places.

Back aching started again!

1 Peter 4:12, 13 (NKJV): Beloved, do not think it strange concerning the fiery trial which is to try you, as though some strange thing happened to you, but rejoice to the extent that you partake of Christ's sufferings, that when His glory is revealed, you may also be glad with exceeding joy.

October 7, 2013

Prophecy: New Cycles of 7, (Description of Our New Home), Land, Little girl standing to the left of the house, wearing pink, black, and white. Significant Weight Loss, 14 Years of Marriage: First 7 Years – Plenty, Prosperous, Second 7 Years – Famine, New Cycle. Sent you to CTW to be prepared in the spirit for the famine. Write the Book! Read it again until you 'Become' the Book! Will give you Power and Revelation through your own book! Don't leave out the details! Book: Most Holy and to be reverenced, 60 days. "Don't doubt anything I've told you, daughter!" You wavered but convinced yourself. Praying for women and saying: "If God Birthed a Miracle in me, He'll birth one in you!" Host Conferences. "I will make you smile again!" Anniversary, Happiest Ever! Removing cradle robbers and back stabbers. By the mature age of 70, you'll understand the "Cycles of 7" in your life.

October 20, 2013

My aunt was the guest speaker in Macon at VDEC. She ministered from Exodus Chapter 30 about the "Anointing" and the process of making the oil. It was awesome! (You'll see the connection in just a second.) We have to go through the process to receive our anointing!

October 21, 2013

Prophecy: Increased Night Vision, Increased your own faith voluntarily. Going to show you some things that you weren't ready to see five months ago, Allowed you to Fortify (strengthen, protect, secure) your Rank in the Kingdom. Will cause you to walk amongst Generals: Self Promotion! Nothing Affects You Anymore! Extracted as in the process of the anointing, (the olive is pressed and extracted to get the oil out, previous prophecy.) You have passed your test! The Greater the Call: The Greater the Trial! Healing the Spiritual Blood Disease in the Family, September 2014. Like the Breaking of Day, Tony will live again: 2% left to get out of him. This season of warfare is over!

October 22, 2013

The Holy Spirit revealed to me: "You have been extracted as the olive, which is the final procedure in the process!" I started writing the book today!

(February 25, 2021: Just thought about the time I inquired of God about coming off the cross and I heard "22" which could signify when I began writing this book.)

October 25, 2013

Prophecy: Your Greatest Feature is Your Faith! Pray in the Spirit before going to bed, More Discernment, Your Revelations will be given in the Night Seasons, especially concerning Business. Don't wait in silence too long! Joseph Prince, Year of the Open Womb! Cassia from the tempered part of China, used in making the anointing oil, has to be imported—imparted. Claim your territory: A love worth reclaiming (Tony): Be careful of bragging rights!

A few of my students were talking about doctor's offices, and I heard one of them begin to speak about Women's Health of Augusta's new office. This is the first doctor's office I went to in 2005 and again in 2012. A few of the doctors there also delivered Keelan in 2002. I felt God was giving me the signal to make an appointment, but when, I didn't know! Finality, the reality of what's final: What I've waited eight years for is finally reality!

October 27, 2013

After hearing the message at church today, I made the decision to call and schedule my appointment. The message was from:

Mark 5:29 (NKJV): Immediately the fountain of her blood was dried up, and she felt in her body that she was healed of the affliction.

I believe that it's time for Manifestation! I believe that when I call on tomorrow, my appointment will be scheduled for November 18, 2013!

October 28, 2013

Called to schedule an appointment, and it was scheduled for November 19, 2013 at 9:50 AM. Rod Parsley was talking about the Shunammite Woman on his television show. She was the woman who the scripture was speaking of when I got in the car after leaving the doctor's office in 2005. ***I heard the Spirit say to me,*** "Your Faith is Your Seed, Your Seed is Your Faith!" While I was writing and reading over the book, the number "22" came up again! I'm sure it will be revealed in due time.

November 3, 2013

This is not the season to run behind people. If they leave, let them leave! And don't let people walk with you who are not willing to cut some things off for the sake of Kingdom Business and Purpose. Elijah passed by and Elisha left his family to follow him, (1 Kings 19:20-22).

"Kiss and Cleave"

Jesus said to the disciples:

Luke 9:23-26 (MSG): Then he told them what they could expect for themselves: "Anyone who intends to come with me has to let me lead. You're not in the driver's seat—I am. Don't run from suffering, embrace it. Follow me and I'll show you how. Self-help is no help at all. Self-sacrifice is the way, my way, to finding yourself, your true self. What good would it do to get everything you want and lose you, the real you? If any of you is embarrassed with me and the way I'm leading you, know that the Son of Man will be far more embarrassed with you when he arrives in all his splendor in company with the Father and the holy angels.

In this walk of Faith, you have to deny yourself to find your "True" Self!

November 9, 2013

Spent the majority of the day cleaning and having the boys clean up as well. Kameron had a problem doing what he was told to do, so he called Tony and left the house. I called Tony and asked if Kam called him. He said yes and immediately started taking his side, not knowing the whole story. When Tony got to the house, we had a major blow up. We both said some hurtful things. It got worse than it ever had in the past. He took my phone and wouldn't give it back. I was so fed up that I told him those awful three words, "I Hate You!"

I kept repeating it, over and over. I don't think I've ever said that to anyone before in my entire life! I also told him that I was releasing him from the marriage. I don't want him, God! I'm tired of holding on to something that wants to be let go! "I'M LETTING GO!"

Later that night when I laid down in bed, I felt a strong KICK! So, I burst into tears. It was as if "SHE" was saying: "I'm still here and I'm getting ready to come out!" God, I'm so ready for this to be completed!

November 10, 2013

Prophecy: Watch out for cunning craftiness: Strange Battle Uphill. You're walking toward the sun with a silver shield, you smote the enemy with the light from the reflection of the shield, from every side: Because the "Son" will surround and protect you on every side. Bounce Back, Building a wall around you! Grace and Glory! You've chosen to walk in righteousness: Not moved to the right or left. A bear coming towards you, but he's gentle, so it's not what appears evil. Watch out for what tries to come from behind. Keelan will speak some interesting things in the next few weeks. Overpass: Something will overpass you, good! Different Realm, Stay on guard, you're in the Spirit. Will take you places in the Spirit and give you a tour of your life. Philanthropist: Promoter of all things good! The Season you're in: Two Types of Weight: Bad or Dead, You discern the one and God will judge the other. He's causing you to cast things aside. You've passed through the Valley of Weeping!

> *Psalms 24:3-5 (NKJV): Who may ascend into the hill of the Lord? Or who may stand in His holy place? He who has clean hands and a pure heart, Who has not lifted up his soul to an idol, Nor sworn deceitfully. He shall receive blessing from the Lord, And righteousness from the God of his salvation.*

This describes where you are! The Hill represents the Strange Season. This is a battle that you have to fight as Moses. "Where I'm taking you, you feel like you're going alone: Come up to the mountain!" Holy Ground! Sharpen to Edify: Tongue will become sharp in this season. People will want to think you're being mean, but they won't because they'll know it's God! Depart from Lot, Abraham. The curses of generations will not be saved, but because of your intercession, Lot will be saved! When he comes out, nothing will be attached! You're Moses, Abraham, and David in this season. The weight of this battle is over. Rest from the War Zone! Will refresh you and make this season about you. Too expensive: Handwriting on the wall, show you things you've never seen before as Daniel.

I had a dream that the boys and I were on a broken-down ship with dangerous waters below. We used a rope to swing from the ship to get to the shore without going through the water.

(Back aching for the past few days!)

The Calm Before The Storm

November 19, 2013

My doctor's appointment was today! I arrived at 9:45 AM. I saw the same doctor from my last visit, and I explained to him that I was still having the same symptoms. He examined me and said for the second time that I have an enlarged uterus. I also had another Vaginal Ultrasound—Revealing Nothing! This time I asked the sonographer if the ultrasound could detect anything in the fallopian tubes, "She said no." So, I asked the doctor what procedure could be performed to check my tubes. He told me about the HSG X-ray. He thought I wanted to check my tubes to see if they were open so I could get pregnant, so he told me to call and schedule the procedure if I wanted to have it done... to be continued.

November 22, 2013

Tony's back with a 180-degree turnaround! Giving 100%! Loving, Kind, and Disciplinarian! We went to the movies to see "Best Man

Holiday" and it was the best movie I've seen all year! It spoke to me in so many ways and on so many levels: The book writing, forgiveness, the hair loss (mine has been shedding a lot), and most of all, the baby girl at the end of the movie! I cried so much watching this movie that I was still crying when we left the theater! Tony kept asking me if I was okay. I was doing my best to hold back the tears.

November 23, 2013

Olaundra dialed my cell phone by accident at 5:42 AM, which was really no accident. I talked to her for a few minutes about the movie and thanked her for recommending that we go see it. When I went back to bed, Tony was awake as well. Neither one of us could go back to sleep, so we began talking about the movie again. I explained to him why I was crying so much. First about the baby girl that Harper and Robin had since they'd been trying for so long. Even though we were not trying or expecting to have another child, the fact that it is a promise from God was enough reason to keep the faith and endurance!

Secondly, I finally told him about the book that I'm writing. He even read the first few pages. I then asked him if he believed me this time and he said, "Yes!" I asked him a few times as we were talking to respond with a little more detail, and these are the three phrases that he spoke at different times: 1. "Amazing!" 2. "It Is Well!" and last but not least, my man of few words said… 3. "It Is So!" We are finally on one accord and in full agreement with the "Plan of God" for this family! Time for Manifestation to take place!

December 3, 2013

I called to schedule the "HSG X-ray" yesterday. I waited for them to call me back and they called today. It's scheduled for tomorrow at 9 AM. I told Tony that I was nervous about going and having to go alone since he couldn't get off work. He started preaching to me about fear and trust, and the Promised Land! And to really sum it up, he said, "At least they're doing something they've never done before, so we are moving forward!" Great way to put it, "Shut me right up! When a generally quiet person speaks, listen up! Something 'Powerful' is about to be said!"

December 4, 2013

I'm here at the Outpatient Center of the hospital about to have an HSG X-ray. A Hysterosalpingography: a procedure in which a red dye is injected through the cervical canal and watched on an x-ray screen to check for spillage in both fallopian tubes. If the dye spills out the other end of the tube, it's open. If the dye doesn't spill out the other end of the tube, it's not open or is blocked. Tony prayed for me before I arrived. I went into the waiting room and took a seat, after filling out the proper paperwork. I started typing in my journal on my iPad.

Shortly after, they called me back. As the procedure began, I turned my head towards the screen and looked for about 30 seconds, but because it was so painful and uncomfortable, I turned my head rather quickly to try to bear the pain. I heard the Radiologist say, "There is definitely spillage from the right tube but not the left." He then asked me to roll over to my right side to get a better picture of the left side, then vice versa for the other side. I believe he asked me to turn to the other side to throw me off and keep me from wondering why he was looking at one particular side. Then they started speaking to each other in medical terminology that I didn't understand. It was Very Painful, but very quick! It may have lasted every bit of 5 minutes.

As I sat up, the doctor said to me, "There is one tube clear, the right one, and all you need is one, so that's good news." I'm laughing to myself because even if they spotted something abnormal, they wouldn't tell me right away. The doctor said they'd get back with me once he and the Radiologist looked over the x-rays. I was done and out of there by 9:30 AM.

December 27, 2013

So, I had the HSG X-ray on December 4, over three weeks ago, and I haven't received a phone call yet! While getting my nails done, I decided to call. I explained to the nurse that I was calling about the results of my procedure. She then tells me that only the doctor can give those results and he'd call me back in a few. As soon as my nails were done, the phone rang. I walked outside and answered. It was the nurse! She says, "Ms. Moore, I am calling to let you know that the results from your procedure were normal. Everything was clear!"

So, I said, "Normal? Were both my tubes clear?"

She responded, "Yes!" By now, I'm very puzzled but slowly said, "Okay," and ended the call.

Clearly, something was wrong with this picture! First of all, I was told that only the doctor could give results and second, I heard both the doctor and the radiologist say that my left tube was not clear! I wanted to call and ask questions, but I felt the need to be Patient and Wait!!!

I'm learning to wait on The Lord and not rush anything! So, the answer is: No, we're not quite there yet!

Temporary Turbulence

Now we are well into 2014. My husband left again for the seventh time in April. This time, I told him to leave because he'd been sleeping on the couch for over a month with no intention of addressing our issues. One issue was, as it so often has been, setting order in the house. We were having a conversation about the boys being more responsible: getting up on time, cleaning up after themselves, etc. And once again he took it that I was blaming him even though I was saying "we." I am also aware that this process I'm going through is also causing an issue in our marriage. Help Us Lord!

May 18, 2014

Prophecy: 6 Months of Rest! Get what you need to get and get out of there. The fulfillment of your 'True Identity' is not in the building but in the Exiting! Destiny and a Makeshift Meeting, Great waters rise up against you. "Seek Me: You will not Fear, Flee, or Forget My Promises. In your day of trouble, I made My Promises Good, Acceptable, and Perfect!" Will hide you in a cloud by day and fire by night! You will transcend! Transported light years in advance, ahead of where destiny needs you. Get your 'Law Degree' together! You are a Governing Authority to Reign in the Earth: Promoting Goodness, Wellness, and Health! Arrival, New Arrival, and Arrival is coming! Unveil the mystery of the dates, Ending of The Book!"

July 21, 2014

I'd been praying for direction concerning my job. A director's position that I filled as an intern came open in April, for which I was highly qualified for. Well, to make a long story short, it was given to someone who didn't even meet the minimum qualifications. I asked God what happened, and He reminded me of what He said, *"Overpass: Something will overpass you, good!"* He was preparing me to exit. I heard Dr. Trimm and a Pastor discussing 'Rejection' being used to push you into Purpose! July 2, 2014, was my last day. I told Tony prior to him coming home that I was leaving my job. He seemed to be fine with it, initially. I actually met Dr. Trimm in Macon on May 31, 2014. I gave her my business card and asked if she needed a personal stylist to travel with her.

Prophecy: Going to do something Amazing and Spectacular, Surprise, Not Forgotten! The Completion of 2 becoming 1.

August 7, 2014

Prophecy: No more delays, setbacks, or long hauls. 90 days: (Nov. 6). I will meet My needs; I have met My need! Tony: November 23.

August 8, 2014

Stayed up all night with the Holy Spirit speaking! I couldn't go to sleep. Ke'Lani was overturning, moving, and kicking repeatedly! I woke Tony up, put his hand on my stomach, and he actually felt movement for the first time! Shawn is the only other person who's ever felt movement. (Been listening to Bill Winston: "The Law of Confession"—Prophecy Fulfilled: Law Degree!) Started back writing the book since I'm not working!

September 1, 2014

Prophecy: Birth your husband in the Spirit: Now, it will turn in your favor. Unleavened bread revelation, Washing him with The Word! Whisper and watch God fight our battles. You're walking on water. Faith for Nations. You will have a Greater Anointing and Witness: Greater understanding from others. September 1 – November 23: Birthing Season. Don't sit and get too comfortable: Destiny before purpose! Attacks are not by chance. Stay in the place with God: Producing Glory in You! Allowed the enemy to come against you to Produce a Weight of Glory! Do Not Doubt Where You Are! Your Ministry is greater than your school: can fund the school. Attraction to Dr. Trimm's anointing because your ministry is likened to hers. You have The Spirit of Wisdom! Prepare for a Vineyard: Harvest Is Coming! The last seed you sowed brought you out and to another realm of Faith and Revelation. Breathe Life to The Vision! Breaking every wall in your life: A New You! Not going to look like where you came from. Strength, Strength, and More Strength! Anointing you with Favor, New people, Kingdom and Business Minded, Strategy: Work the system (Law of Confession) and it'll work for you!

September 16, 2014

Tony came in last night and again went to the sofa. Once again, I told him if we couldn't pray and discuss the issues, he needed to leave. He's not been back a full three months, and he's gone again, but didn't take anything with him.

September 29, 2014

I ministered this past Sunday a message titled "The Power of Words." As I was in prayer today, I heard the Spirit of the Lord say: "I'm Bringing Destiny to You!" He's speeding up the process. The Set Time Is Now! "You Manifest Miracles!" He has given us the power and authority to do Greater Works! We often say we are waiting on Him, when He is waiting on us to "Discover Who We Are!" Jesus said:

John 14:12 (NKJV): "Most assuredly, I say to you, he who believes in Me, the works that I do he will do also, and greater works than these he will do, because I go to My Father…"

September 30, 2014

While typing the book, I had a glimpse of the future God has prepared for us. I began weeping with joy! I'm so grateful to be chosen by The Almighty! Indescribable!

October 8, 2014

I had a dream that Tony, Kameron, and I were crossing over into enemy territory. They came after us, but Tony and I ended up in complete unity and harmony.

Almost immediately after the dream, I had problems almost every day with Kameron's behavior (he was 14 at the time). From being disrespectful and rebellious, to lying and failing grades! He even went as far as sneaking off to a party when he was supposed to be at a game. He was in full-fledged defiance! I knew this was an attack from the enemy. We prayed, talked, I punished him, snapped a few times, you name it, I tried it! But nothing was working! I called Tony on several occasions, but that didn't work either. It actually drove a deeper wedge between us, which was exactly what the enemy was aiming to do. He was totally out of control. I had to call on several people to talk to him. I was completely stressed out and unfocused on my assignment. (Fluid leaking and back aching)

October 24, 2014

Back aching intensified! I attended a Prophetic Conference and of course I was the first one called out.

Prophecy: Your Faith has stretched in this season. You know what God said and you're standing and not moving! You don't care who doesn't understand! Surprises are coming! God is connecting the pieces to the puzzle. And Tony: Call his name out: God is arresting him right now, where he is! He's going to call you.

November 3, 2014

Prophecy: Things manifesting before mid-December. God is wrapping your Faith in His Glory! His Glory will produce miracles. Reiterate Chapter 17 (this book originally had chapters): dream, buildings, and the sky looking weird and unusual. No more sick and impoverished finances. Empowered to Prosper, Empowered to change!

November 4, 2014

I read Chapter 17 again, and right after the part about the tornado, it talked about when I went to the doctor. Particularly the "Original Doctor's Office" from 2005. So, I already know what that means! I called and scheduled an appointment with the same doctor I'd seen the past few times after. My appointment is set for November 13th, at 8:10 AM. When I heard, "You don't need a doctor," it was because I needed Faith! Now that my Faith is in full effect for The Promise, God's Glory will carry me to Completion and Manifestation!

November 6, 2014

Prophecy: (90 and 30 days) I went to bed last night with a MAJOR headache: I know I'm stressed! I woke up this morning with the same headache and tightness in my chest! I couldn't even get out of the bed to see the boys off to school. I was so tired and drained emotionally that I slept all day until 2:00 PM! I got up, cooked, and listened to Jesus Culture as I have been for about two weeks now. I went and picked Kameron up from practice at 6:30 PM.

In the car, I told him I didn't feel well, and I was not up for any discussion or debate about anything. I was very quiet. When we got out of the car, I heard him ask Keelan what was wrong with me. I went into the house, fixed his plate, and sat down at the computer. I still had Jesus Culture playing, and he asked if he could turn it off and turn on the TV. I politely said no. He started rapping and making his normal weird noises, so I asked him to please stop. After he finished eating, I told him several times to go take a shower and go to bed. He insisted on being disobedient.

After having to deal with this for months now, I felt myself on the edge. I told him one more time to go upstairs and he wouldn't. So, I charged at him, fell, and grabbed him and he bumped his head on the cabinet. He still wouldn't go upstairs. Even Keelan kept trying to get him to go. As I was talking, crying, shaking, and could barely breathe, God revealed what was happening and I began explaining it to him. Because I was playing worship music constantly in the house, the atmosphere was set, a demonic presence manifested as a result! It was time to kill this demon attacking my child once and for all!

After explaining it to him, I asked him if he wanted to change. I walked the floor, anointed the doors, and prayed in the Spirit. I told Kameron that he could go stay with his dad or he could denounce rebellion, manipulation, and anger because no more was allowed in the house! He said he wanted to denounce it. I told him, no rap music and he must read his bible in the mornings. Once all of this was over, my headache was gone, and my heart was no longer heavy!

Sometimes our prayers are answered but held up by demonic forces that the angels contend with in the spirit realm. Keep praying and pray without ceasing.

> *Daniel 10:12-13 (NLT): Then he said, "Don't be afraid, Daniel. Since the first day you began to pray for understanding and to humble yourself before your God, your request has been heard in heaven. I have come in answer to your prayer. But for twenty-one days the spirit prince of the kingdom of Persia blocked my way. Then Michael, one of the archangels, came to help me, and I left him there with the spirit prince of the kingdom of Persia.*

November 8, 2014

Holy Spirit reminded me about Tony coming home on the 28th. I wasn't sure if it would be the 28th of November or December but when I looked at the clock, at that moment it was 11:28 AM! (Stay tuned because that date is very significant, August 28, 2019.)

The Inevitable Storm

November 10, 2014

Found out that a great General, Dr. Myles Munroe and his wife died in a plane crash yesterday! He has been and still is an inspiration and a major voice in my life, growth, and understanding of The Kingdom of God.

"Wrapping your Faith in My Glory," from Faith to Faith and Glory to Glory! At a heightened level of Faith, God's Glory covers you. This is when you are ready for Greater Works: Miracles, Signs, and Wonders!

November 12, 2014

Your purpose will not be hindered or delayed when it's hidden in God! Worked on typing the book for the majority of the day. Finished everything I'd written in my journal. Now I have to summarize 2014 and the prophecies. Waiting for the end of the book. Doctor Appointment in a few hours at 8:10 AM. Good night! 1:42 AM.

November 13, 2014

Arrived at my doctor's appointment. Listened to my favorite song Oceans by Hillsong, on my way there. Sitting here now in the waiting room.

So, I see the doctor and all he says is I have three options depending on if I have fertility concerns. I told him that I did not have fertility concerns. He recommended birth control pills, hormone supplements, or some mild laser procedure. I have no cysts, fibroids, or polyps. He checked my cervix, I told him I'd think about the options, and I got out of there so fast! He did say he knew that I'd been dealing with this for a while now. He was talking about heavy cycles, which is not the problem at hand. So maybe I just had to go one last time for the record!

God, You know exactly what You're doing and I trust You!

Had to call back to schedule my yearly exam since he didn't do it while I was there, so I still have to go back on November 20 at 1:30 PM.

Prophecy: Don't toil or weep over the harvest the enemy planted, the tare growing with the wheat. Nothing can penetrate the wall of fire around thee, the wheat and the tare, I have allowed to grow together. The harvest is not in vain. For I have not forgotten or turned my face from thee. I have hidden thee. Just about in the last hour around midnight, it will come forth, beautiful and glorious. Iron weights and heavy chains, I have appeared unto thee twice and will again.

I have walked through thy house and made a pathway even in thy kitchen. Jesus is watching you! You've reached the apex of the mountain. This is the altitude that you must reach to wave and dive in My Glory! Fear not, neither fret for I've heard thee in the midnight hour. I've awakened thee at 2 AM, 3 AM, and 4 AM. I will bring shame to thine enemies. To the watery grave, baptism! Dying to self, that which dies shall live again. For mercy has prevailed and the enemy's plan has failed. Defeated the enemy long before you were born. Your ending is prepared, Glorious! Don't let the weight of the world drag you down. Conquer in faith!

Thy light shall appear, My Glory shall appear! I've seen thy due diligence. I will promote thee in the midst of the banner and the waving of the flag. Surrender: white flag, sweet surrender. Enemy: red flag, cannot defeat sweet surrender. I will coat thy wounds with ointment. Thy heart has been penetrated with more than ten thousand suns in brightness and glory. For thy shame, double! The enemy will no longer ride over your head but under your feet. Never move from the place of provision that I have called you to!

I am your Shepherd, you shall not lack. I have not caused you to prosper in the land of pharaoh just to bring you to famine again. You will receive wealth unheard of! I have sent my angel with the trumpet before you. Get going with the business! Be clear on what I've called you to do and stay focused. You've alienated yourself from pleasure. I have not forgotten what is in thy womb to bring forth. I have spoken it from my mouth. Harken unto me in due diligence. I'm wiping my hands clean of it. Baby in a bonnet. Reposition thyself: The burden you carry is too heavy! I'm going to lighten the load.

Prayed in the spirit before bed: (Shield) Back aching and fluid leaking.

November 15, 2014

I went to see Olaundra in a play tonight while the boys were with Tony at a basketball tournament at the high school. I got home after them, gave instructions to clean up, get clothes out, and be in bed by 11:30 PM. Kameron made a "hmmp" sound and after months of dealing with his disobedience, I'd had all that I could take! I told him to get out and that he could no longer stay there. He called his dad, and of course he took Kam's side as he often did. I told Tony to come and get him. He then told me that he'd come when he was finished doing what he had to do, since I did what I wanted to do earlier.

So, since he wanted to play that game, I unplugged all the phones in the house and wouldn't answer his calls. I packed up all of Kameron's things and threw them downstairs! All of a sudden, Tony shows up, grabs my cell phone, and puts it in his pocket. I told him to give my phone back, and I reached for his pocket to grab it. As he snatched away forcefully, I stumbled and slid across the kitchen floor. I told them to leave, but they kept slowing around. He told me he was going to have me locked up and put in a mental institution. He said out loud, "Nine years and she still thinks she's pregnant!"

Keelan and I packed up a few things and headed to my parent's house. We got here after midnight.

Prophecy: Every spirit of violence and rage is gone, devils and demons have I chased that you may live again. Unveiling, you will hear those things again, from Tony. Open up the treasure of your heart and let your mouth speak forth good things. Edify yourself in spirit. Look up scriptures every night about how I feel about you. Psalm 139 and Proverbs 31: Read for the next 30-45 nights and write what you feel. Will produce a 'Book of Love' to help people understand My

Love. There's more on Love! Seasons passed, will never pass this way again!

Give specific instructions, strategy, and wisdom. Five specific areas I'll show you in scenarios. You teach in parables. I know the way you take, Time Traveler. Will cause you to leap in the spirit, dimension to dimension. Going to put portals in your path. The crooked will be made straight and the rough will be made smooth. There are five doors in front of you, not a bunch of space like in a house: Door to door without the hallways! My promise and the promise: You said you're not going to waver in faith, so I'm not going to waiver in My promise! Did not I say if I spoke it, shall I not make it good? New direction of overflow, another place. Your adverse situations will be obsolete, standing at the foot of the cross and in My Glory! Sid Roth: It's Supernatural, Glenda Jackson was talking about Angels with shields. Thursday night, as you prayed in the Spirit, I put a shield in your hand. As I'm piercing the heart, I'm washing. You'll know in the morning.

November 20, 2014

Dr. Appointment 1:30 PM: Walking down the hallway saying, "I can't mess this up! Lord, You've got this! It's already done. Thank You Jesus! Whatever happens, it's still already done!" Sitting here now, waiting to be called back.

So, I had my cervix checked, and the Doctor asked had we done an ultrasound? I told him yes; I had one done a while ago. When he came back in the room, sat down and asked me what my thoughts were. So once again, I explained to him about the movements and sensations I've been feeling. I also told him that I'd tried everything I knew to do and didn't know what else was to do. He assured me that he didn't think it was gynecological, and that I probably need to see a

Gastrointestinal Specialist. THEORY: "I Still Don't Need A Doctor!" To be continued…

November 21, 2014

Tony called around 3:30 PM to talk to Keelan. At first he told Keelan to tell me hello, then he asked to speak to me. He apologized for what happened that night. He told me that he's going to give me back the house key and my cellphone. He asked why we haven't gone home yet. I told him it was just a lot that happened that night, and also that I was praying for him and Kameron. Then I gave him my new phone number. He told me that he was praying for all of us, and that he didn't want us to think that he was a bad person. I told him we didn't think that at all. We'd gone five days without talking: Temporary Discomfort for Permanent Change!

November 22, 2014

11/22 it's 2:22 AM and I'm still up: Thinking about the day I prayed and asked God when could I come off the cross and He clearly said 22!

2:15 PM: Back aching

6:45 PM: had a few flashbacks of waiting and being disappointed in times past.

7:50 PM: feels like my cervix is opening up, a little pressure down below. Fluid leaking a little.

8:30 PM: Back feels like it's on fire up my spine like an epidural.

8:50 PM: Breast aching and frequent urination.

12:33 AM: Nothing's happened yet, I prayed and cried, so tired and ready for the process to be completed!

I miss my family, and I'm ready to go home. Please Hear My Cry Oh Lord! This is very hard, but nonetheless, I must endure hardship as a good soldier! I Love You Lord! I was very emotional throughout the night.

November 23, 2014

I went to church today; it was a little hard at first, but once I went inside of the building, I was fine. Worship was awesome! Fluid has been leaking a lot. I had a talk with my pastor, I was glad he reached out to talk to me. We discussed his concerns and his questioning of my hearing from God. I told him that I respect his concerns, however my spiritual walk is not "normal" because of the call of God on my life. A Great Call = Great Trials! I told him most people won't understand and that all things will be revealed in due time!

I decided to get out of the house and go for a drive. Keelan told me to tell God he said, "Hey," and to provide for us! My child knows me well enough to know I'm going to have a talk with Jesus. I drove around the outskirts of the city a few times while praying. I felt warfare going on, and I also received another prayer language. I felt some things move and shift in the spirit. Went back to the house and told Keelan God said, *"Tell him I said Hi!"*

November 24, 2014

Talked to Kam and Tony about what happened that night. Kam apologized, and so did I. I told Tony that Kam still couldn't come back home unless he came with him.

You Don't Need A Doctor, Remember?

November 25, 2014

1-2 AM, Researching Ectopic Pregnancies, specifically abdominal: hard to detect, normally from a ruptured tube. I've been having severe abdominal pain on my right side. I need to have an MRI or CT Scan. I called to schedule an appointment with the specialist and was told that I'd receive a call back.

November 26, 2014

Called the doctor's office and talked to two different people. One lady said: "Oh, this has been going on for too long. Have you heard from someone in Triage?"

I told her no, I hadn't, and she put me on hold and transferred the call to the appointment desk.

The second lady said, "They haven't contacted you yet?" She then put me on hold to call the specialist's office and said, "They are closed today and probably Friday, too. We'll call you Monday to get you an appointment if you haven't heard from them."

So, I asked for the specialist's name, thinking it was a Gastrointestinal Specialist. She told me the specialist's name. I looked her up and found out she's an OBGYN High-Risk Pregnancy Specialist. I'm perplexed at this point!

December 2, 2014

Got a phone call from the doctor's office. The nurse started questioning me about my being referred to an OBGYN. She said, "That's for women who are pregnant and you're not."

I told her that she needed to speak with the doctor about that and if that's who he referred me to, that's who I need to see. She then tells me that he has a note that I have Gestational Diabetes in my file. I told her, I absolutely do not! She said she'd talk to him and call me back. No call back as of close of business.

December 3, 2014

I got a call from the doctor's office at 12:44 PM from someone totally different saying the doctor doesn't recall talking to me about a specialist, only about NovaSure. I told her that he'd mentioned a gastrointestinal specialist, but it was fine and not to worry about it. She then told me that I could call one without a referral.

So now I'm like, "Lord, what do You want me to do? Every time I feel like I'm getting close to a resolve, I get knocked back!" Crying, "Lord guide me, do I not do anything and just wait? But I refuse to go into another year with this unresolved! I TRUST YOU! I've come too far to keep getting stuck!"

So, I looked up information to request my medical records, and I called the other doctor's office to see if they'd already sent the referral, which they had not. So, what next? 1:44 PM, I called to tell the nurse that I needed to talk to my doctor about the information I'd been receiving over the past few days. I'm waiting on a call back from him.

When he called back at 2:17 PM, I explained to him the inconsistent info I'd received. He apologized and said he'd mistaken me for another patient with a similar name. I then asked him about the results from the HSG X-ray that I'd never gotten. He proceeded to tell me that my left tube showed spillage, which is normal, however my right tube seemed to spasm, which is totally in reverse of what he said right after the procedure. I then told him about the severe pain I'd been having on my right side and that I wanted to rule out an ectopic pregnancy. He told me that it could be ruled out with an HCG blood test and to come by the office and request a test at any time, no appointment needed. (I had a blood test back in July 2005)

I cried for about thirty minutes! Lord, what do you want me to do? I can't go back there! I feel like I've sacrificed my family, my home, my career, everything! I need You to do it: Reveal it! I surrender, I've done all I know to do! I'm waving my flag!

9:30 PM: Back still aching. I'm going to pray from direction on whether to go get the blood test tomorrow or Friday. Tired of being disappointed!

December 4, 2014

Read in the Book of Genesis before going to bed. I meditated all night on Genesis 15:5-6 (Imputed as righteousness) and 18:14 (Is there anything too hard for the Lord?)

December 5, 2014

Went to the doctor at 8:45 AM to have another HCG Blood Test. They are going to call me with the results.

December 9, 2014

Still cleaning and preparing. Prayed in the Spirit for about an hour. Back aching and my side is hurting more often, especially when lying down on my right side. (Typing this on December 10, 2020 and my side is currently hurting.)

Prophecy: Watching for specifics of deliverance in Tony, by the 19th, 23rd, 24th, 28th day. The Parliament of Heaven: Angels, Speak and will veto even the land on your behalf. Give me liberty or give me nothing at all: Request honored! Make me a cake. Marriage License Still Intact. Voice Recorder: picks up sound, Voice Command: picks up, plays back, and commands an action! This season vs last season: you feel Daddy's God's Love! Filtered the Voice Recorder. Title Wave of the Command, Crash and Collide into Destiny.

January 13, March 14-28. Pureness of your praise brings God's Glory! The weak spot in your flesh will be healed! Tender around this time of year. Takes a lot of faith to believe for promises. Time well spent lately. The Lord sees me! Time is not wasted or lost but redeemed, the submergence of obedience. Said you won't go into a new year with the same issues. Soothsaying of the witchcraft has been blocked. Kameron: will see a change in his speech, heart, and attitude. Manually shifted him in the spirit. In your hands and you shifted it. Shifted to the last gear and no reverse, only forward from here.

Kingdom, past six weeks and past six months, new revelation of your journey. Genesis 13:17 (land), Secret Treasures in Hidden Places. Yes: I will sweep the nation with your feet! Be careful of what you say about people's deliverance because it will draw nigh. Hidden Wisdom and Revelation, Seasons of Seven: Years of The Lord! Will not return void. Your life decision making, not wrestling or struggling. Supernatural Wisdom of Apostles. Those in the House will know. Faith and Wisdom will produce Power! Wisdom, signs, and wonders. Football pads on Tony's shoulders, weighty mantle: Will revenge his faith! Enemy tried to steal his measure. Teaching Faith vs Defending, seasons to come with family members. Will welcome your Faith: Appointing you over hewn stones to make lively stones. (February 26, 2015, same prophecy confirmed)

December 12, 2014

Song came on the radio as I was riding in the car, "Be Born In Me" and oh how it spoke to my spirit! This promise is greater than I realized. Listened to it several times as it inspired me in a major way. Be it unto me as thou wilt, oh Lord! A few hours later, I got a call from my aunt that she and my uncle wanted to meet with me a few days before Christmas. Then Tony drops Keelan off after getting his haircut and doesn't even come in to speak. Kam walks in on his phone and doesn't speak. I'm so tired and ready for this to be completed! I want to be loved and respected. To top everything off, it's been a week and I haven't heard anything about my results from the blood work yet! How much longer, Lord? Please don't let me down! But somehow, I know You won't! I'm going to focus on Keelan's birthday tomorrow and make sure he enjoys it!

December 15, 2014

Took the blood test on December 5, but no results yet, so I finally called them! Results: NEGATIVE! Ok, I held it together this time and said, "God, what do I do next?"

I remembered reading about the MRI. So, I searched online to see if I could have one done at the Urgent Care Facility or the Emergency Room. I can't just keep sitting around waiting for something to happen: Faith without works is dead! Order My Steps Lord!

Prophecy: Sequence of Events no longer a delay, Full Reciprocity! I have heard your prayers, a lot you've been praying about, and He's been praying through you. Increased faith through the preached word, but I want you to understand. Competency of Wisdom: through observation of how and when He moves! Strategic in His Supreme Being. Everything I do is like an affair or event. Will cause you to comprehend My Building Blocks (thought process, foundation of Christ, The Word). A Just Weight, Proverbs 16:11, Honest weights and scales are the Lord's. All the weights in the bag are His work (concern), my business is His business. Did I not say: "The *Household* of Faith will be revived through your faith?"

December 16, 2014

While getting ready to come to Prompt Care this morning, I had a sharp pain shoot through my right shoulder. So, I got ready a little faster. Arrived here at the Grovetown Office just before 9 AM with no one in the waiting room. I told the Rad Nurse about all of my symptoms and everything my doctor had checked. The nurse came in and seems to think it is gallbladder related—Certainly not! She is ordering me to have a CT Scan. Waiting now. The CT Scan is scheduled for 1 PM at Evans Imaging.

12:15 PM: Leaving home, heading to get the CT Scan.

They called me to the back while preparing the room and gave me a warm and cozy blanket. I only waited about 10 minutes, went into the scan room around 1:30 PM and was headed to my car at 1:38 PM. They are going to fax the results over to the Prompt Care doctor who will then call me. Thank you, Jesus, I'm at peace because I know in my spirit that it is the Finality!

December 17, 2014

I called several times and finally got an answer around 4 PM. The results showed nothing but a possible cyst on my spleen that could be causing the pain. They are referring me to a Gastro-intestinal Specialist. Lord, I really don't want to go to another doctor, but Your will be done!

December 18, 2014

So, the Gastro center called to schedule an appointment but had nothing available until January 22. I told them that I would find another doctor because that date was too far out. So Lord, I'm leaving it in Your hands. I don't want to do anything that You haven't led me to do. So, I'm not moving until you speak!

I looked up the words Dynamic and Resolve and came across the word Endoscopic which stood out to me. Ok Lord, I'm still trusting You, I've come too far, and I have a lot on the line! Everyone is looking at me like, "What are you going to do?" Even Tony! I'm asking You Lord to speak to me in a dream, as I sleep and that I remember clearly what You want me to do, if anything.

December 19, 2014

Had a dream this morning that I was actually in a Baby Store walking around looking at bottles and bibs but not really doing anything. I saw my aunt but didn't say anything to her. I saw a few other people I knew as well. I remember being in the store just looking around from 8:30 AM until 1 PM. So, I didn't call or do anything.

December 24, 2014

I had a three-hour meeting with my aunt and uncle about my past, my marriage, my personal relationships, and my birthing experience! They still don't quite understand why I still believe, and I'm okay with that. They prayed with me and had me renounce some things and people. Lord, I'm still trusting that You are about to finish this process that's already done! Emotional: Lord, I know You are able to deliver me! Why haven't You yet?

December 27, 2014

Studied Ingredients in preparation for my products. I had a moment where I just laughed and said, "There is no way You'd let me go out like this! Incomplete and defeated with no victory—No way! You don't operate like that at all! Especially in front of a few unbelievers that I know. No! I'm sorry Lord for doubting You! I know people are watching."

December 31, 2014

I realize that I love me, and God loves me more! So, He would not let me go through this being totally deceived! I refuse to come out empty handed! I have too many people watching and depending on me! Lord, please finish this! I refuse to go into another year like this! If you don't deliver me before tonight is over, I Give Up!

YOU DON'T HAVE TO FORCE WHAT GOD HAS ORDAINED
Summary of 2015-2019

January 1, 2015

Very emotional! Still feeling kicks, so You didn't remove or stop anything because of my emotions. My faith is still intact, however I'm really tired and ready for this all to be settled! I don't wish this feeling on anyone! I'm going into a season of isolation. I already have a new phone number, anyway.

January 3, 2015

As I was heading back to my parents' house, I passed the spot where I completely surrendered my all to You Lord. This was the spot that I told God to use me however He wanted to and that I was a willing vessel submitted to His will for my life.

At that point of surrender is when it seemed as if All Hell Broke Loose In My Life! As I drove by, I started to feel again. My eyes began to tear up as I'd been numb for the past few days.

January 6, 2015

I told Keelan that I was going to apply for a job and he asked, "Did God tell you to do that?" After thinking about what he asked, I realized that God didn't tell me to, so I told Keelan, no. He then says, "I would've been mad if you did and God didn't tell you to. It's like you're giving up on Him if you do that!" I was so lost for words that it brought tears to my eyes.

January 8, 2015

New beginnings, my focus shall be and stay on You, Father! You've already handled my affairs! Thank You Lord. My prayer today: Whatever you have for me will find and chase me down! I call it to myself!

Prophecy: Priesthood is a Lifestyle of Worship: Fourth Watch, Tony, closure of negative during this separation. Confirm His Word with Signs Following, Mark 16:20. You are in the place with God, The Hidden Place: Go Deeper!

I received so many prophetic words that led up to what was about to take place, yet I still was not prepared for what was coming!

During the year 2015, after years of back and forth, up, and down, our marriage as we knew it, of over fifteen years ended in divorce. Tony filed sometime at the end of 2014, and I knew nothing of it. He made hints of it at times but never told me he filed. This was the most devastating thing that ever happened to me, even more so than the birthing process I was going through that I didn't fully understand. We had been trying to work things out, so I thought, for the early part of 2015.

In March, I was served the papers and was completely caught off guard. I never responded to, acknowledged, or signed any documents sent because I knew the will of God and what He'd spoken to me about our union. I was finally summoned to court in April 2015.

As we walked from the parking lot coincidentally at the same time and entered the courthouse, Tony looked at me with uncertainty in his eyes. I couldn't believe he was actually going through with this. He spoke to me and asked how I was doing. I spoke back but looked at him like, "Are you seriously asking me that right now!"

As we went into the courtroom to go before the judge, I looked over at Tony and his lawyer and then looked at the empty chair beside me, as I had no lawyer, but I did have a representative! I placed my purse in the chair and turned it with the cross faced outward. Jesus was sitting at my right side that day. The judge asked if I had anyone representing me and if I had anything to say, so I told him no (even though I really did) and that I recommend Faith Based Marital Counseling. I told him I was not willing to make a permanent decision based on temporary circumstances!

The judge asked Tony if he would agree to counseling. Tony looked at him and responded, "I want a divorce!" This was definitely not the response I was expecting after just seeing him with the look of uncertainty a few minutes prior.

Now what I didn't know is that Teresa texted me at the exact time I was in the courtroom on my old phone that I'd left home. We hadn't talked in a while and she didn't have my new phone number. So, she definitely had no idea about the court hearing or even the thought of divorce. Her text message read, "Hi. You never have to force what God has already ordained. :-) I love you. God bless."

I fought every idea of this divorce going through. I just knew God was not going to allow the enemy to take it this far. But guess what? He allowed it! Seven days later, the divorce decree was signed by the judge. At that moment I went into total shut down! I went "off the grid" onto my own Island of Patmos for about six months.

I was embarrassed, ashamed, and broken. Not just because my marriage was over, but also that my family was torn apart and that the promise had yet to be fulfilled. During that season of shut down, I came to know God in me, in an even greater way! Also B. Well by Kenisha was birthed. Olaundra allowed me to stay at her house during the day while Keelan was in school. It was truly a cave and hiding place where I sought peace during that time.

The Year 2016 was about me focusing on my healing and growth. There were a few people that God had in my life during this season, including my cousin Katesha, whom I've always been close to and a good friend I met, that really helped me through the healing process. There were a few others that helped unknowingly as well.

During this process of healing, I learned to love on a greater level. I realized I was in love with the idea of marriage and family, but truly didn't know how to love someone for who they were.

2017- 2018

I tried the dating scene briefly, and that was very interesting to say the least. I even married someone else briefly, and that failed. You see, the entire time, I was in the process of healing and trying to move forward by not thinking about Tony or the Promise, but they both were in my spirit so heavy that I still couldn't completely shake it.

After my short-lived marriage, which didn't even last one year,

Tony apologized for the hurt and pain he caused over the years. He felt that what I went through with the second divorce was also his fault, even though that was definitely not his fault. But the reality was that God had a plan far greater than what he and I could even foresee.

We both realized that we were destined to be together. I knew it before we divorced, but I appreciated him on a totally different level after going through a second divorce. And him seeing me move on (well, try to move on) opened his eyes to God's original intent for us.

"You never have to force what God has already ordained."

Tony and I remarried August 28, 2019, which was our original wedding date, August 28, 2009. Our end signified a new beginning! (Prophecy Fulfilled: Tony coming home on the 28th)

All Praises To The Most High God!

PERFECT VISION
20/20

Everyone was excited as we crossed over into the year of 2020: Proclaiming it to be The Year of Double, The Year of Perfect Vision, The Year of Change! Vision and Change is exactly what happened. When the pandemic hit, many of us were sent home from our jobs in March, and change really began to take place as we transitioned into a new way of life. My 2020 vision kicked in and I set my face like a flint to focus on what truly mattered. Hindsight really became 20/20 for me through reflections as revelation knowledge began to set in.

I think most of us began to realize the true value and importance of life, family, and a true relationship with God. Which reminds me of a dream Teresa told me she'd recently had about Tony and me, where she heard God speak this phrase to us, "PURPOSE OVER EVERYTHING!" This happened right at the time God was dealing with me, again, about leaving my job. I'd built over a twenty-year career as a Cosmetology Educator and for the fourth time, God was pulling me away from it. It was definitely time for me to put 100% of my focus on my Purpose. Teaching over the past twenty years was a preparation for my TRUE Purpose. As I walked away from my career, thinking it was because of the pandemic and everything that was going on, I knew deep down in my spirit God was preparing me for something greater!

Just about everything I'd prayed for in the previous years continued to manifest in 2020. Tony and I built our first home, started a Ministry, "The Unveiling," and God also divinely connected us with mentors to help push us into the next realm of glory. One of those connections was with Kaishia, who helped pray and push me through the process of finishing this book, as I'd been stuck for a while. I truly thank God for her gift and willingness to assist. I also thank her for being able to see what God was doing in me without judgement! There is so much more to come, and Tony and I are truly thankful to God for choosing us to be carriers of His Presence in the Earth.

And to finally sum up the birthing process, for those of you who have been waiting for it, here's what happened:

One day while a friend and I were worshipping God, the Glory of The Lord showed up mightily. I began to speak what He was saying, and before I knew it I was laid prostrate on the floor and I clearly heard Him say to me, "I WAS BIRTHING YOU!"

You see, the MAIN purpose of me going through this process was to birth *Me*. Yes, Tony was birthed (pull the baby out of the oven by the head), Businesses have been birthed, Ministries have been birthed, but the ultimate SEASON OF BIRTHING was about GOD Birthing Me! Through this Birthing Process, I have discovered not only my purpose but also MY POWER! I was UNLOCKING MY OWN POWER throughout the process and GOD HAS EQUIPPED ME TO ASSIST YOU IN UNLOCKING YOUR OWN POWER!!!

This process has made me strong on so many levels; even though I was wrong about some things, because I leaned on my own understanding and tried to make things happen myself. I believed God with all my heart and STILL believe that He can birth a miracle child through me if He wants to! There's still more because the kicking is STILL there. I wholeheartedly Trust Him, Unwavering and Undoubting! Stay Tuned for Whatever Else I Am Birthing, however, until then, LET'S UNLOCK YOUR POWER!

A SEASON OF BIRTHING *Unlocking the Power Within*

PART 2
The Power Keys

UNLOCKING THE POWER WITHIN

The Power Keys

As God revealed He was birthing me and I was birthing my power, He gave me Eight Power Keys to share with you! These are the Keys I gained access to, after each phase in the process of unlocking my power. My Assignment is to make you aware of your access to these keys, by restoring priority to your hidden potential, resulting in Realigning you with Your Purpose. In this section, the words you are about to read, will be planted as seed that will take root in your spirit! Once you go through your own process that God has designed specifically for you, You Will Receive a Harvest of Power, Unlocking Your Power to Pursue Purpose!

Power Key #1
The "Yes"

Definition of YES: noun - an affirmative reply, adverb - used as a function word to express assent or agreement.

The first Power Key is the most important of them all. It is a sign of total Surrender. Without it, many people go haphazardly through life with no real plan or since of purpose. This particular yes that I am speaking of, is not the yes that was your affirmative reply at the time of Salvation. That would be a necessary prerequisite before you can even completely comprehend "The Yes" at hand to begin unlocking your power. However, let's stop right here and address anyone reading this right now that has not expressed the initial Yes for salvation.

Repeat this prayer and make sure you believe what you are speaking:

Lord Jesus, I know that I am a sinner, and I ask for Your forgiveness. I confess with my mouth, and I believe in my heart that You died for my sins and rose from the dead. I repent and turn away from sin and invite You to come into my heart and be Lord over my life. I will trust and follow You. I receive You as my Lord and Savior. Amen!

Awesome! Now that we've gotten the first yes affirmed, let's finish discussing what I like to call The Second Yes! This is the Yes in response to the Call from God that you heard in your spirit. No one literally asks you anything. You'll just respond to a question that God has presented to you: WILL YOU SURRENDER TO MY WILL?

You'll have a knowing in your spirit when this proposition takes place. For some of you that moment JUST happened as you read those words. This silent, but very loud question, sometimes hits you like a ton of bricks suddenly and unexpectedly. For me, it happened when I was driving home from work, if you remember, as I recalled the moment in *Part 1 The Journal*.

The response or affirmative reply to God's question goes a little something like this: *Yes, Lord, I surrender to Your will for my life. I will do whatever You want me to do, go wherever You want me to go, and say whatever You want me to say! Not my will, Lord, but Your will be done!*

It's not always exactly in that manner, but that's an idea of what to expect when it hits you. You are agreeing to sacrifice what you want, for what He wants for you. This is the ultimate sacrifice that you, as a free will human being, can give to The All Seeing, All Knowing, All Powerful God! You really can't go wrong; however, it's not necessarily going to be an easy process. It wasn't even a few weeks after I expressed the "Yes" that it seemed as if my life began to go in a downward spiral, thus the dream about the airplane that gracefully descended into a crash, but we landed in a beautiful body of water. This is the process of dying that you must go through in order for Him to live in you and operate through you.

Read the following scriptures out loud and then repeat the "Yes" Prayer & Declaration to give your Affirmative Reply when you're ready.

Galatians 2:19, 20 (NKJV): For I through the law died to the law that I might live to God. I have been crucified with Christ, it is no longer I who live, but Christ lives in me, and the life which I now live in the flesh I live by faith in the Son of God, who loved me and gave Himself for me.

Matthew 16:14, 25 (NKJV): Then Jesus told his disciples, "If anyone would come after me, let him deny himself and take up his cross and follow me. For whoever would save his life will lose it, but whoever loses his life for my sake will find it.

James 4:7-10 (MSG): So, let God work His will in you. Yell a loud no to the Devil and watch him make himself scarce. Say a quiet yes to God and He'll be there in no time. Quit dabbling in sin. Purify your inner life. Quit playing the field. Hit bottom, and cry your eyes out. The fun and games are over. Get serious, really serious. Get down on your knees before the Master, it's the only way you'll get on your feet.

Prayer & Declaration: Abba Father, as I surrender my will to Yours, give me the strength, courage, and endurance to go through whatever is necessary for me to fulfill Your Purpose in my life. I trust You wholeheartedly through this process that You have designed just for me! Amen!

Power Key #2
Obedience

Definition of Obedience: noun - compliance with an order, request, or law or submission to another's authority.

Definition of Obey: verb - carry out (a command or instruction).

Definition of Submission: noun - an act or instance of submitting or yielding control to a more powerful or authoritative entity.

The second Power Key is Obedience, which requires Full Submission to God's authority. It is the willingness to comply with the instructions given and also the process of being respectful, yielding to order. Obedience to God's commands is a sure sign of your love for God. You have to know His Word in order to know how to walk in obedience. When you act in obedience, you are willing to carry out the plan of God for your life by any means righteously necessary! This requires complete confidence and total trust in God.

Definition of Confidence: noun - full trust, belief in the powers, trustworthiness, or reliability of a person or thing.

When He begins to deal with you about the assignments and purpose of your life, you can't always share with others what He shares with you—Joseph! Not everyone will understand because He didn't reveal it to them because it was for YOU!

The bible tells us that Obedience is better than Sacrifice. God would rather have your obedience than outward signs of sacrifice and worship. Actually, Obedience is a type of sacrifice that is pleasing to the Lord. Another test of ultimate sacrifice is: Will You Obey What You Don't Understand? As I was going through my process, I walked in obedience, even when I didn't completely understand what I was obeying. All I needed to know was Who I was obeying—God! This definitely requires a confidence that is almost supernatural.

Now, the balance that I now have, compared to then, is totally different because I am not trying to make something happen in my own right. In other words, I stopped trying to *control* the situation! Obedience requires relinquishing Control, the main enemy of Submission!

Definition of Control: verb - to exercise restraint or direction over, dominate: command.

God puts people of authority in our lives as well, to help us learn submission. So not only are we to submit to God, but also to those in authority over us and to one another. This is the part of the process that teaches you Humility. You can be confident and humble at the same time. The confidence that I am speaking of is confidence in God, not in one's self. I now understand why, "The Only Way Up Is Down!" It teaches you how to remain humble so that once you come up, you are able to sustain your new position. You'll be less likely to do anything to jeopardize it.

Definition of Humility: noun - freedom from pride or arrogance: the quality or state of being humble.

PART 2 *Unlocking The Power Within* | *Power Key #2: Obedience*

Read the following scriptures out loud and then repeat this Prayer & Declaration of Obedience as an act of Submission to the process.

Romans 12:1, 2 (MSG): So here's what I want you to do, God helping you: Take your everyday, ordinary life—your sleeping, eating, going-to-work, and walking-around life—and place it before God as an offering. Embracing what God does for you is the best thing you can do for him. Don't become so well-adjusted to your culture that you fit into it without even thinking. Instead, fix your attention on God. You'll be changed from the inside out. Readily recognize what he wants from you, and quickly respond to it. Unlike the culture around you, always dragging you down to its level of immaturity, God brings the best out of you, develops well-formed maturity in you.

John 14:23 (VOICE): Anyone who loves Me will listen to My voice and obey. The Father will love him, and We will draw close to him and make a dwelling place within him.

1 Samuel 15:22, 23 (MSG): Then Samuel said, Do you think all God wants are sacrifices—empty rituals just for show? He wants you to listen to him! Plain listening is the thing, not staging a lavish religious production. Not doing what God tells you is far worse than fooling around in the occult. Getting self-important around God is far worse than making deals with your dead ancestors. Because you said No to God's command, He says No to your kingship.

Philippians 2:7, 8 (NKJV): but made Himself of no reputation, taking the form of a bondservant, and coming in the likeness of men. And being found in appearance as a man,

He humbled Himself and became obedient to the point of death, even the death of the cross.

Prayer & Declaration: Father God, as I begin to walk as Jesus did, in full Obedience to Your will for my life, I relinquish control, submit to Your authority and those You have put in authority over me, and I confidently put my trust in You! Holy Spirit, lead and guide me into All Truth. Amen!

Power Key #3
Faith

Definition of Faith: noun - strong belief in God or in the doctrines of a religion, based on spiritual apprehension rather than proof.

Biblical Definition of Faith: Now faith is the substance of things hoped for and the evidence of things not seen (Hebrews 11:1).

After discussing complete trust and confidence previously in the Power Key of Obedience, it leads us right into our third Power Key: Faith. Equally important, Faith and Obedience are parallel in the process of unlocking your power, as it takes Faith to operate in Obedience. Faith in itself is an actual real substance. It's not just a non-tangible, hoping and wishing for something to happen that never happens. It's an Invisible Reality!

Definition of Invisible: adjective - unable to be seen, not visible to the eye. Examples: sound, energy, gas, feelings, thoughts, etc.

There are countless things that are invisible to the human eye, but that does not mean they don't exist. We don't physically see God (besides in you and me, but that's another subject), however, we know He exists by Faith. Just because you can't physically see something, does not mean that it's not there. Faith is an assurance that what I see in the realm of the spirit will eventually manifest in the natural realm. And actually, for those of us who operate in the Gift of Faith, we already see it in the natural before it manifests or becomes visible.

Now the question is, *How do we obtain Faith*? We are all given a measure of faith, and it's up to us to build on that measure and increase our faith. How do we build our Faith? The bible teaches us that Faith comes by hearing the Word of God. The more we hear The Word and study Jesus, The Word, we'll get a better understanding of God's ways and His Character. Our Faith in Him increases the more we get to know Him. In our relationships with people, we don't often have faith in those we don't know on a personal level. So, the more personal you become with God, the more He reveals to you, definitely resulting in greater Faith in Him.

Now the Gift of Faith is not the same as the measure that we all receive. While all believers possess some amount of faith, there is a gift of faith which is a special ability to trust God beyond the limits of what we think is normally possible. Not every believer possesses this spiritual gift. Those with this gift have a trust and confidence in God that allows them to live boldly for Him and manifest that faith in mighty ways.

In the Bible, the gift of faith is often accompanied by great works of faith. Holy Spirit distributes this gift to some members of the Body of Christ to encourage and build up the people. Those with the gift of faith take God at His Word and believe that the impossible is possible! They expect God to move and are not surprised when He answers prayers or performs miracles.

The most difficult part of my process was Building My Faith. However, just as it was difficult, it became easier over time. It was difficult, only because I kept trying to do things in my own strength. I was trying to force the situation to go the way I thought it should go, and in the timing I thought it should happen.

What made it become easy? Every time I tried to waver in my faith, quit the process, or give up, God always reminded me of the things He'd shown me and spoken to me. Because of my faith, willingness, and obedience (the first three keys), He was in constant communication with me throughout the process.

Even when others mocked and doubted me, my Faith was getting Stronger because God kept sending me reminders. Every time I felt like I'd been knocked down, I got back up with a Force of Power that was inexplicable! I became fiercely determined and relentless to see this process through, all the way to the end! And guess what: I STILL AM!

The difference between where I am now versus then is, I don't have to know all of the details of what God is doing, nor do I have to completely understand everything. My Job is to TRUST and BELIEVE! Which will also be Your Job as you go through Your Process. It should be a little easier for you since I already told you what I did wrong so you can avoid those mistakes.

Read the following scriptures out loud and then repeat this Prayer & Declaration of Supernatural Faith to do the impossible!

Hebrews 11: 1-3 (NLT): Faith shows the reality of what we hope for, it is the evidence of things we cannot see. Through their faith, the people in days of old earned a good reputation. By faith we understand that the entire universe was formed at God's command, that what we now see did not come from anything that can be seen.

Romans 4: 20 (NKJV): He did not waver at the promise of God through unbelief, but was strengthened in faith, giving glory to God.

Romans 10:17 (NKJV): So then faith comes by hearing, and hearing by the word of God.

Romans 12:3 (NKJV): For I say, through the grace given to me, to everyone who is among you, not to think of himself more highly than he ought to think, but to think soberly, as God has dealt to each one a measure of faith.

2 Corinthians 5:7 (NKJV): For we walk by faith, not by sight.

1 Corinthians 12:8-10 (NKJV): For to one is given the word of wisdom through the Spirit, to another the word of knowledge through the same Spirit, to another faith by the same Spirit, to another gifts of healings by the same Spirit, to another the working of miracles, to another prophecy, to another discerning of spirits, to another different kinds of tongues, to another the interpretation of tongues.

Hebrews 11:6 (NKJV): But without faith it is impossible to please Him, for he who comes to God must believe that He is, and that He is a rewarder of those who diligently seek Him.

Prayer & Declaration: Lord Jesus, As I have Faith in You and what You did on the cross for me, Strengthen My Faith to help me complete this process and to believe that You have given me the ability to do greater works! I expect miracles, signs, and wonders to follow me because I believe! Holy Spirit endow me with the Gift of Faith as necessary for the fulfillment of my calling and purpose in this earth! Amen!

Power Key #4
Observation

Definition of Observation: noun - an act or instance of noticing or perceiving, an act or instance of regarding attentively or watching, the faculty or habit of observing or noticing, an act or instance of viewing or noting a fact or occurrence for some scientific or other special purpose.

Definition of Watch: verb – a: the act of keeping awake to guard, protect, or attend. b: a state of alert and continuous attention. c: close observation: surveillance.

Definition of Discernment: noun - the power of discerning, keen perception or judgment, insight, awareness.

It's time to explore the fourth Power Key, Observation. You may ask, "Why is observation important?" Well, this is the phase of the process where we need to pay attention to details, watch and pray, so to speak. Realize that what you are carrying is so precious, it has to be protected by any means necessary. And don't be naïve and think that everyone is excited about your process of becoming! This is far from the truth.

The next question may be, "What am I watching?" Everything.

Absolutely Everything! Be watchful and observe your surroundings: watch what you intake and consume, watch who you allow in your presence, and watch out for distractions. It is very important to be observant naturally, but definitely spiritually. Tony gets on to me from time to time about not paying attention to my surroundings. I would always make the excuse of, "I'm not that observant." When in all actuality I realized, I am more observant in the spirit than I am naturally. This is where Discernment kicks in.

Discernment is a decision-making process in which an individual makes a discovery that can lead to future action. In the process of spiritual discernment, Holy Spirit guides us into making the best decision. Now, I didn't always use proper discernment throughout my process, especially when I kept going to doctors when God clearly told me I didn't need one from the very beginning. As time went by and I grew in wisdom, knowledge, and understanding, my discernment increased. So, make sure you *Grow through the process as you Go through the process*.

You shouldn't allow everyone in your ear trying to give you advice about your situation. Remember, God revealed it to you and not everyone else. It's okay to receive Godly counsel, however no one's voice should be louder than God's voice, not even yours. And last, but definitely not least, watch the enemy who is watching you. If we are more aware of what is going on, we won't be so caught off guard when the weapons form. We'll be fully prepared with our Whole Armor that we should already have on, anyway.

There were times that I literally had to fight for what I believed, not physically but spiritually. When really, I was only fighting my flesh, which was filled with doubt! The battle doesn't belong to us, anyway; it belongs to God! And technically you already have the victory before you even enter the fight! I eventually discovered that Spiritual Warfare trained me to be tough and bold in the spirit; however, eventually I didn't have to fight as much: I JUST HAD TO BELIEVE!

Read the following scriptures out loud and then repeat this Prayer & Declaration of Observation and Discernment to protect your promise!

Ephesians 1:18, 19 (MSG): I ask—ask the God of our Master, Jesus Christ, the God of glory—to make you intelligent and discerning in knowing him personally, your eyes focused and clear, so that you can see exactly what it is he is calling you to do, grasp the immensity of this glorious way of life he has for his followers, oh, the utter extravagance of his work in us who trust him—endless energy, boundless strength!

Matthew 26:41 (VOICE): Now maybe you're learning: the spirit is willing, but the body is weak. Watch and pray and take care that you are not pulled down during a time of testing.

Romans 12:2 (VOICE): Do not allow this world to mold you in its own image. Instead, be transformed from the inside out by renewing your mind. As a result, you will be able to discern what God wills and whatever God finds good, pleasing, and complete.

Ephesians 6:11-13 (NLT): Put on all of God's armor so that you will be able to stand firm against all strategies of the devil. For we are not fighting against flesh-and-blood enemies, but against evil rulers and authorities of the unseen world, against mighty powers in this dark world, and against evil spirits in the heavenly places. Therefore, put on every piece of God's armor so you will be able to resist the enemy in the time of evil. Then after the battle you will still be standing firm.

Prayer & Declaration: Holy Spirit, help me to become more aware of my surroundings, spiritually and naturally. I speak and believe that I am walking in a greater level of discernment. I walk in full authority with my armor on, protecting the promise that You entrusted me with! Amen!

Power Key #5
The "Wait"

Definition of Waiting: verb - stay where one is or delay action until a particular time or until something else happens.

Definition of Patience: noun - the will or ability to wait or endure without complaint. Steadiness, endurance, or perseverance in the performance of a task.

Definition of Endurance: noun - the ability to keep doing something difficult, unpleasant, or painful for a long time.

Here we are, already at the fifth Power Key! By now you should already feel a stirring in your spirit to discover what is locked inside of you. Some of you may be thinking, "I already know who I am." Well guess what, There Is More! As we discuss the process of waiting, we will look at the benefits of waiting, as well as the drawbacks of rushing through the process.

First of all, our process is designed specifically for us. The Father knows exactly what it will take to shape and mold you into who He's called you to be. So don't ever despise your process or question someone else's process. No matter how long it takes or what you have to go through, Trust God all the way through. God could have easily told me, "*I AM Birthing You,*" from day one when my process began. However, He allowed me to go through it the way I did for a reason. He knew what it would take to build my Faith, Boldness, Endurance, Tenacity, and POWER!

A major benefit of waiting is the development of Patience. By letting her have her perfect work, you learn to go through the process without complaining. You eventually get the gold medal of Endurance by staying the course, even when it's tough and painful. This is why I say don't ever question or judge someone's process just because you don't understand it. Trust me when I say, "It Is For A Reason!" Everything is not the devil, sometimes things that look strange are God at work!

There were many nights when I was saying, "Take this cup from me, nevertheless, not my will…" Endurance always kicked in. Waiting doesn't have to be hard. If we really knew what our process was preparing us for in the future, we'd embrace it, nurture it, and enjoy the journey. The joy of the waiting in the process comes from knowing that you are changing and evolving into your True Self!

Every time we complain or try to take matters into our own hands, we prolong the process. Just like the children of Israel did, as they kept complaining and were disobedient after their freedom from the bondage of Pharaoh in Egypt. If you know the story, they caused an eleven-week journey to turn into forty years. So, complaining and disobedience is definitely a drawback, an enemy to progress. This was the second hardest part of my experience. I kept trying to control everything. I was so impatient that God allowed me to experience disappointments to teach me several lessons.

Rushing through anything in life can cause unnecessary mistakes.

If I am baking a cake in a hurry and I accidentally forgot a main ingredient, when it's time to eat it, you'll know something is missing. It won't taste right. If you try to rush your process, you are not going to get the results you want. You see, either way, You Still Will Have To Go Through The Entire Process! If you rush it, you'll birth an Ishmael. This is the result Sarah and Abraham ended up with because of Sarah's rushing the process. If you try to abandon the process, you'll birth a Stillborn! Definitely be careful of going into full rebellion causing a Spiritual Abortion, which is an Intentional Termination of the Promise.

Definition of Stillborn: adjective - (of a proposal of plan) having failed to develop or succeed, unrealized.

However, by enduring "The Wait," you'll birth an Issac! This was God's original plan for Abraham and Sarah. Don't get caught up on how long it may take and how old you may be when it finally happens. Just Endure!

Waiting Patiently signifies that you trust the one in charge of the process. Rushing implies that you still want control and haven't fully relinquished it: Go Back to Power Key #2 and Submit! Not going through the process at the pace it was designed, can cause setbacks and drawbacks, but God in His Sovereignty still allows us to have comebacks!

Read the following scriptures out loud and then repeat this Prayer & Declaration of Patience and Endurance to bring your promise to Full Term!

James 1:2-4 (MSG): Consider it a sheer gift, friends, when tests and challenges come at you from all sides. You know that under pressure, your faith-life is forced into the open and shows its true colors. So don't try to get out of anything prematurely. Let it do its work so you become mature and well-developed, not deficient in any way.

Romans 8:25 (NKJV): But if we hope for what we do not see, we eagerly wait for it with perseverance.

Psalm 27:14 (NKJV): Wait on the Lord, Be of good courage, And He shall strengthen your heart, Wait, I say, on the Lord!

2 Peter 3:8 (NKJV): "But, beloved, do not forget this one thing, that with the Lord one day is as a thousand years, and a thousand years as one day.

Isaiah 40:31 (MSG): But those who wait upon God get fresh strength. They spread their wings and soar like eagles, They run and don't get tired, they walk and don't lag behind.

Prayer & Declaration: Lord Jesus, just as You waited thirty years to begin operating in Your earthly purpose, teach me through Your example how to wait patiently on my time. I will allow myself to be fully developed through my process, I will not rush it, and I will carry my promise Full Term so that I am able to operate in Purpose with Power! Amen!

Power Key #6
Worship

Definition of Worship: verb - reverence offered a divine being or supernatural power also: an act of expressing such reverence.

Definition of Consecrate: verb - to make holy or to dedicate to a higher purpose.

The "secr" part of consecrate comes from the Latin sacer "sacred." Something consecrated is dedicated to God and considered sacred.

Excerpt from Mark Tittley's "A Manual for Worship Leaders"

"Worship is becoming aware of God's presence and responding to His presence with verbal or active expressions of love and devotion." With the concept of the presence of God being so fundamental to worship, it makes sense to seek to gain a fuller understanding of the Presence of God.

(1) Old Testament Words – there are two main Hebrew words: (a) Shachah – which means to bow down, Prostrate, and (b) Abodah – which means to serve a superior.

(2) New Testament Words – there are two main Greek Words: (a) Proskuneo – which means to come forward to kiss the hand, as an act

of adoration, and (b) Leitourgia – which means to serve.

Notice that worship has a dual aspect: (1) An Attitude of the heart, and (2) Actions of service. The definition of worship presented by Ralph P. Martin shows the two aspects, "Worship is the dramatic celebration of God in his supreme worth, in such a manner that His 'worthiness' becomes the norm and inspiration of human living."

Have you ever heard the phrase or song, *I will Worship While I'm Waiting*? Worship is absolutely a vital necessity while going through the "Wait." Worship is not just a one time or random event, it is considered a Lifestyle. Power Key #6 Worship prepares us to live in and acknowledge the Presence of God on a Daily Basis! This lifestyle brings about a deeper place of intimacy with The Father where you discover Oneness with Him! In this secret place, the mysteries of God are revealed.

Definition of Oneness: noun - unity of thought, feeling, belief, aim, etc., agreement, concord. a strong feeling of closeness or affinity, union.

There are so many ways to worship God and express our love and adoration for Him. We do this by way of praise and thanksgiving, the giving of ourselves, our time, and money. Other forms of worship include singing, raising our hands in worship to Him, bowing down or laying prostrate, clapping our hands, and worshiping Him through various forms of dancing.

The Lifestyle of Worship also requires a Lifestyle of Consecration. Prayer, fasting, separation, and sanctification are a few examples of what this should look like. Your focus should be to remain in a constant state of awareness of God's Presence. This includes a daily reminder to yourself that He is not so far away that He can't be reached: HE IS INSIDE OF YOU! I know that sounds very simple, but really dig into the Revelation of what that means! He operates Through You because He is In You! The Healer is in You; The Deliver is in You; The Provider is in You; The Way Maker is in You! Shall I continue? In Him We Live, In Him We Move; In Him We Have Our Being!

The number one prerequisite of Worship is that it's done in Spirit and Truth. You may be familiar with the song that says, "Lord, I Worship You, Because of Who You Are," well, we must Worship Him from our being and the truth of Who We Are! Which means you have to know and understand Who God Is, as well as understand Who You Are, in order to Worship Him!

Understanding Who God Is requires you to Understand His Presence. The Presence of God is indicative of His Omnipresence as well as His Manifest Presence.

Definition of Omnipresence: the state of being widespread or constantly encountered: the presence of God everywhere at the same time.

Acknowledging His Omnipresence is something we should do daily as fellowship with Him. Now His Manifest Presence is what we must seek to encounter Him by way of The Holy of Holies.

Definition of Manifest: display or show (a quality or feeling) by one's acts or appearance, demonstrate.

This is a deeper place of intimacy where His Glory is displayed, shown, or demonstrated, also known as His Shekinah Glory. The Glory Cloud in the Old Testament is an example of his Manifest Presence.

Definition of Shekinah: denotes the dwelling or settling of the divine presence of God.

In this level of God's Presence, often called *The Secret Place*, the secrets and mysteries of God are revealed. A Lifestyle of Worship is the key to entering into and remaining in God's Presence. The number one thing the enemy tries to use to keep us out of the presence is sin. Sin hinders us from entering into His Presence. This is why the Lifestyle of Consecration, as we discussed earlier, is so important. Both of these Lifestyles are imperative in order to receive the next key to Unlock Your Power!

Read the following scriptures out loud and then repeat this Prayer & Declaration of Consecration and Oneness to develop a Lifestyle of Worship to help you live in God's Presence!

John 4:21-24 (MSG): "Believe me, woman, the time is coming when you Samaritans will worship the Father neither here at this mountain nor there in Jerusalem. You worship guessing in the dark, we Jews worship in the clear light of day. God's way of salvation is made available through the Jews. But the time is coming—it has, in fact, come—when what you're called will not matter and where you go to worship will not matter. "It's who you are and the way you live that count before God. Your worship must engage your spirit in the pursuit of truth. That's the kind of people the Father is out looking for: those who are simply and honestly themselves before Him in their worship. God is sheer being itself—Spirit. Those who worship Him must do it out of their very being, their spirits, their true selves, in adoration."

Psalm 16:11 (NKJV): You will show me the path of life, In Your presence is fullness of joy, At Your right hand are pleasures forevermore.

Psalm 91:1 (NKJV): He who dwells in the secret place of the Most High Shall abide under the shadow of the Almighty.

Acts 3:20, 21 (NLT): Then times of refreshment will come from the presence of the Lord, and he will again send you Jesus, your appointed Messiah. For he must remain in heaven until the time for the final restoration of all things, as God promised long ago through his holy prophets.

Isaiah 4:5 (NKJV): then the Lord will create above every dwelling place of Mount Zion, and above her assemblies, a cloud and smoke by day and the shining of a flaming fire by night. For over all the glory there will be a covering.

John 15:1-8 (MSG): I am the Real Vine and my Father is the Farmer. He cuts off every branch of me that doesn't bear grapes. And every branch that is grape-bearing he prunes back so it will bear even more. You are already pruned back by the message I have spoken. "Live in me. Make your home in me just as I do in you. In the same way that a branch can't bear grapes by itself but only by being joined to the vine, you can't bear fruit unless you are joined with me. "I am the Vine, you are the branches. When you're joined with me and I with you, the relation intimate and organic, the harvest is sure to be abundant. Separated, you can't produce a thing. Anyone who separates from me is deadwood, gathered up and thrown on the bonfire. But if you make yourselves at home with me and my words are at home in you, you can be sure that whatever you ask will be listened to and acted upon. This is how my Father shows who he is—when you produce grapes, when you mature as my disciples.

Prayer & Declaration: Almighty God, I acknowledge Your Presence and I declare My Oneness with You. I ask for strength to carry me through the process of Consecration. Prune me and cut off everything in my life that is hindering me from living in Your Presence. I abide in You as You abide in me. I will live in Your Presence where there is fullness of joy and pleasures forevermore! Amen!

Power Key #7
Glorification

Definition of Glorification: noun - the culmination of sanctification.

Definition of Culmination: noun - the highest or climactic point of something, especially as obtained after a long time.

Definition of Sanctify: verb - 1: to set apart to a sacred purpose or to religious use: consecrate. 2: to free from sin: purify. 3: to impart or impute sacredness, inviolability, or respect to.

Definition of Glorify: verb - to cause to be or treat as being more splendid, excellent, etc., than would normally be considered.

From Wikipedia, the free encyclopedia: Glorification (theology): Glorification is the final stage of the ordo salutis and an aspect of Christian soteriology and Christian eschatology. It refers to the nature of believers after death and judgement, "the final step in the application of redemption." [1]Biblical verses commonly cited as evidence for this doctrine include Psalm 49:15, Daniel 12:2, John 11:23-24, Romans 8:30 and 1 Corinthians 15:20. [1]The theological

---
[1] Wayne, Grudem (1994). Systematic Theology. Nottingham: Inter-Varsity Press. pp. 828–839.

doctrine of glorification goes on to describe how believers will be resurrected after death and given new bodies that have a degree of continuity with their mortal selves. [1]The process of glorification is where God removes all spiritual defects of the redeemed. It first involves the believer's sanctification, where they are made and are being made holy, it is a continual process where the Holy Spirit works to mold believers to the image of Christ. Glorification is the end goal of every Christian's life journey.

It's no coincidence that Power Key #7 is Glorification: Seven represents Completion and Perfection. If Glorification is the culmination of sanctification, it also means in simplest terms that Glorification is the pinnacle or apex (highest point) of purification. Also, to Sanctify means to set apart and make holy for a higher purpose. So, after developing the Lifestyle of Consecration and Worship, you are ready and Sanctified for The Master's use.

We have discovered that Glorification is a continual process that goes on until we receive our instant transformation at the last trumpet, when Jesus comes back to rapture us up. Also, the purpose of Glorification is to transform us into the image of Jesus. This is done through the process of Sanctification by way of Holy Spirit. This is why being filled with the Spirit of God with the evidence of speaking in tongues is vital. Sanctification involves one being made holy. This can only be done by the Holy One living inside of you.

At the moment of Salvation through Jesus Christ, you received the gift of The Holy Spirit. So, you are able to consecrate and be sanctified by the Holy Spirit. The process of sanctification is working in us now, moving from one level of glory to another until it reaches final glory. This is why we go from Glory to Glory, because it's a continual process. However, in order to walk in POWER, you need the Baptism of The Holy Spirit and speaking in tongues is evidence that you've been baptized in the Spirit.

God chose you before He made the foundations of this world. He planned long ago who you would be and what you would do. You just have to walk out the plan that is already completed. According to Romans 8:29-30, *He Chose You, Called You, Made You Righteous, and Completed You*! Walk in your glory, completeness and wholeness!

Read the following scriptures out loud and then repeat this Prayer & Declaration of Sanctification and Glorification to be transformed into the image of Jesus and Walk in Power with Holy Spirit!

Roman 8:29, 30 (NKJV): For whom He foreknew, He also predestined to be conformed to the image of His Son, that He might be the firstborn among many brethren. Moreover, whom He predestined, these He also called, whom He called, these He also justified, and whom He justified, these He also glorified.

John 13:31, 32 (MSG): When He had left, Jesus said, "Now the Son of Man is seen for who He is, and God seen for who He is in Him. The moment God is seen in Him, God's glory will be on display. In glorifying Him, He Himself is glorified—glory all around!

2 Corinthians 16:18 (MSG): Whenever, though, they turn to face God as Moses did, God removes the veil and there they are—face-to-face! They suddenly recognize that God is a living, personal presence, not a piece of chiseled stone. And when God is personally present, a living Spirit, that old, constricting legislation is recognized as obsolete. We're free of it! All of us! Nothing between us and God, our faces shining with the brightness of His face. And so we are transfigured much like the Messiah, our lives gradually becoming brighter and more beautiful as God enters our lives and we become like Him.

Romans 8:18-30 (MSG): That's why I don't think there's any comparison between the present hard times and the coming good times. The created world itself can hardly wait for what's coming next. Everything in creation is being more or less held back. God reins it in until both creation and all the creatures are ready and can be released at the same moment into the glorious times ahead. Meanwhile, the joyful anticipation deepens.

22 All around us we observe a pregnant creation. The difficult times of pain throughout the world are simply birth pangs. But it's not only around us, it's within us. The Spirit of God is arousing us within. We're also feeling the birth pangs. These sterile and barren bodies of ours are yearning for full deliverance. That is why waiting does not diminish us, any more than waiting diminishes a pregnant mother. We are enlarged in the waiting. We, of course, don't see what is enlarging us. But the longer we wait, the larger we become, and the more joyful our expectancy.

26-28 Meanwhile, the moment we get tired in the waiting, God's Spirit is right alongside helping us along. If we don't know how or what to pray, it doesn't matter. He does our praying in and for us, making prayer out of our wordless sighs, our aching groans. He knows us far better than we know ourselves, knows our pregnant condition, and keeps us present before God. That's why we can be so sure that every detail in our lives of love for God is worked into something good.

29-30 God knew what He was doing from the very beginning. He decided from the outset to shape the lives of those who love Him along the same lines as the life of his Son. The Son stands first in the line of humanity he restored. We see the original and intended shape of our lives there in Him. After God made that decision of what His children should be like, He followed it up by calling people by name. After He called them by name, He set them on a solid basis with Himself. And then, after getting them established, He stayed with them to the end, gloriously completing what He had begun.

Prayer & Declaration: Lord Jesus, as I continue in the process of being sanctified and glorified, going from glory to glory, to be used to fulfill my call and purpose: Teach me more of Your ways through Holy Spirit so I can become more like You. I understand that I don't have to walk this path alone. I have become a co-laborer with You. So as long as I follow Your lead, I will get to my destination! Amen!

Power Key #8
The Master Key

After affirming your **Yes**, walking in **Obedience** to the call, building Your **Faith**, using intense **Observation**, letting patience have her perfect work in the **Wait**, creating a lifestyle of consecration and **Worship**, and making it to the continual process of **Glorification**: You are now ready to receive the last Power Key to Unlock Your Power!

It should be to no surprise of what the last Power Key, #8 is, as the number eight represents New Beginnings. Of course, it is THE MASTER KEY, which is the obvious. But maybe the not so obvious is that The Master Key is… YOU! Yes, that's right! Once you've done the work and gone through your total process, YOU Have What It Takes to Unlock YOUR POWER to Fulfill YOUR DREAMS, DESTINY, AND PURPOSE! You now have ACCESS to the Key that Unlocks every door that God sets before you. New Beginnings are Waiting on YOU; Awaiting Your ARRIVAL!

JESUS is the prime example and picture of how we should look when we use our Master Key. He already told us that We Will Do Greater Works Than He Did! Your process is designed to get you to the Greater Works. Back in 2001, I remember when I would pray and ask God for Miraculous Power. I would ask Him, *"Where are the miracles, signs, and wonders?*" I've always had such a burning desire to not only see more, but to do more! I just became aware of the entire process: A Season of Birthing, which lasted over sixteen years, was preparing me for what I asked God for twenty years ago!

The Process didn't begin right away. I asked in 2001, it began in 2005, after I affirmed the "Yes." As I've said before, my process was designed specifically for me, as yours is designed for you. God knew exactly what it would take to get me to where I am now. If every Dream, Vision, Prophecy, and Sign of a little girl was God Showing Me Carrying Myself, then so be it! Also, if an actual little girl is born in the future, then so be it! At the end of the day, I am just a vessel. Who am I to tell God how to do His Job? I still don't have to know all of the details! I just Trust Him with my whole being, which is In Him anyway! HalleluYah!

Every Tear, Heartache, Disappointment, Embarrassment, Betrayal, and Separation was worth it! IT WAS ALL WORTH IT! I am not ashamed of anything I've gone through. Because of it, My Faith is Supernatural, Mountain Moving, Water Walking (if He bids me to come) Faith! All because of the Process that I said YES to. Each Power Key that God gave me to give you, is what I also walked through myself. I'm not telling you to do anything that I haven't done myself and am still doing. And if you ever need me, I'll be available to encourage you through your process as well.

Final Declaration: I AM THE MASTER KEY! I UNLOCK MY POWER FROM WITHIN! I AM POWERFUL! I AM BOLD! I AM BRAVE AND I AM STRONG! I AM A FORCE TO BE RECKONED WITH! And Because HE is I AM!

GOD IS US AND WE ARE HIM! Until you truly understand that

revelation, you will not operate in your full power, which is HIS POWER IN YOU!

GO IN POWER! But before you go, I have an assignment for you. After you've gone through your process, gaining access to each power key, and obtained The Master Key that you've really had all along but just needed the Activation to access it, answer this: WHAT ARE YOU GOING TO DO WITH ALL THAT POWER?

Years ago, before my process even began, God illuminated this scripture to me as instructions on What To Do With My Power:

Luke 4:18 (NKJV):
"The Spirit of the Lord is upon Me,
Because He has anointed Me
To preach the gospel to the poor,
He has sent Me to heal the brokenhearted,
To proclaim liberty to the captives
And recovery of sight to the blind,
To set at liberty those who are oppressed.
Your Assignment is to find out what He wants you to do?
Then, GO IN POWER: IN JESUS' NAME!

> *Ephesians 3:20, 21 (AMP): Now to Him who is able to [carry out His purpose and] do superabundantly more than all that we dare ask or think [infinitely beyond our greatest prayers, hopes, or dreams], according to His power that is at work within us, to Him be the glory in the church and in Christ Jesus throughout all generations forever and ever. Amen.*

www.ingramcontent.com/pod-product-compliance
Lightning Source LLC
Chambersburg PA
CBHW071434160426
43195CB00013B/1896